Contents

1

Waitangi

Why Waitangi is a special place

Important Places In Our Past

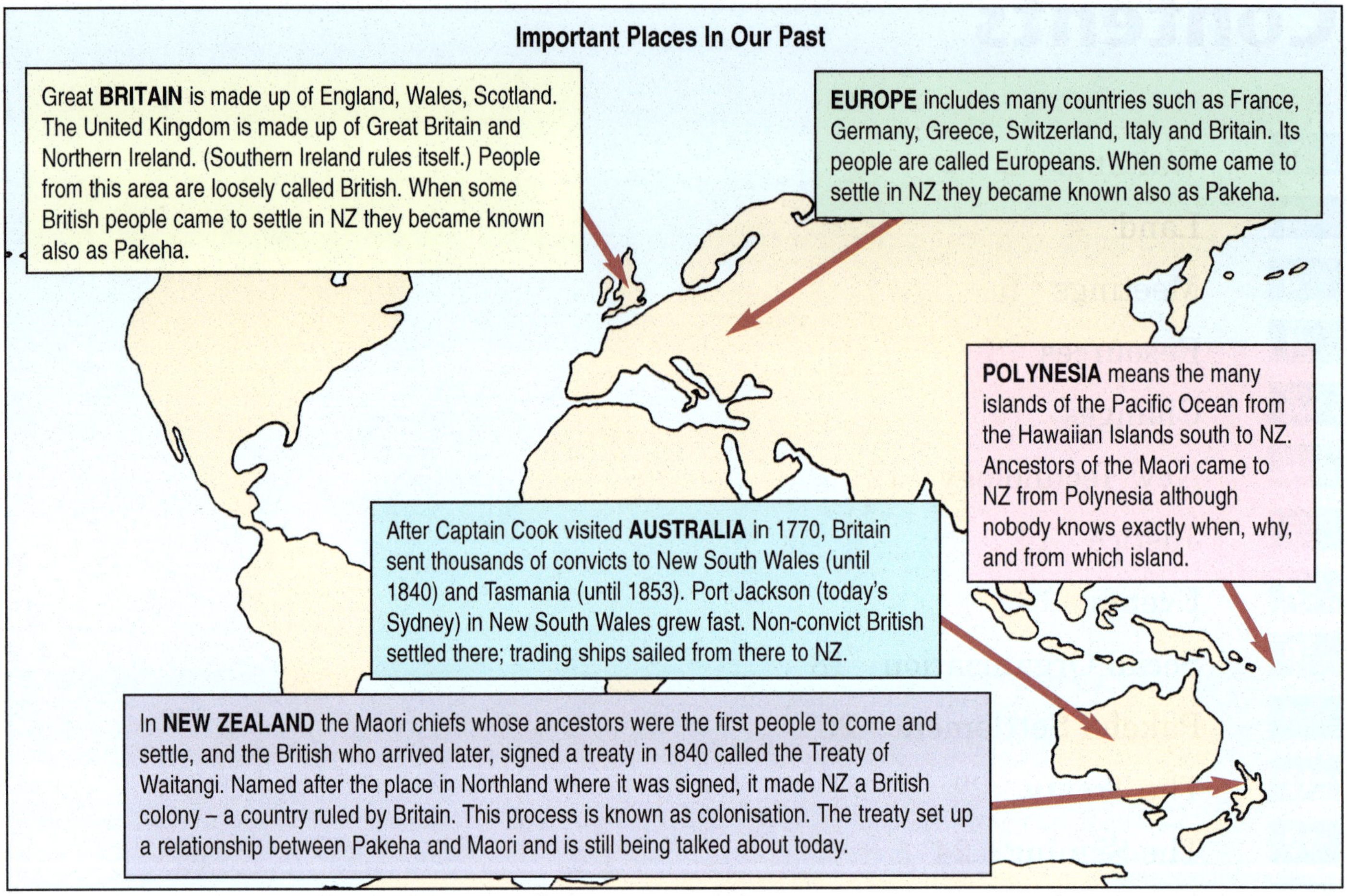

Great **BRITAIN** is made up of England, Wales, Scotland. The United Kingdom is made up of Great Britain and Northern Ireland. (Southern Ireland rules itself.) People from this area are loosely called British. When some British people came to settle in NZ they became known also as Pakeha.

EUROPE includes many countries such as France, Germany, Greece, Switzerland, Italy and Britain. Its people are called Europeans. When some came to settle in NZ they became known also as Pakeha.

POLYNESIA means the many islands of the Pacific Ocean from the Hawaiian Islands south to NZ. Ancestors of the Maori came to NZ from Polynesia although nobody knows exactly when, why, and from which island.

After Captain Cook visited **AUSTRALIA** in 1770, Britain sent thousands of convicts to New South Wales (until 1840) and Tasmania (until 1853). Port Jackson (today's Sydney) in New South Wales grew fast. Non-convict British settled there; trading ships sailed from there to NZ.

In **NEW ZEALAND** the Maori chiefs whose ancestors were the first people to come and settle, and the British who arrived later, signed a treaty in 1840 called the Treaty of Waitangi. Named after the place in Northland where it was signed, it made NZ a British colony – a country ruled by Britain. This process is known as colonisation. The treaty set up a relationship between Pakeha and Maori and is still being talked about today.

Waitangi National Reserve is important because it is:

- a beautiful place
- popular with overseas tourists
- in 'the winterless north' and has a great climate
- in the area where some ancestors of the Maori settled when they came to NZ
- in the area where the earliest Pakeha settled when they came to NZ
- where the Treaty of Waitangi was signed in 1840
- where some of NZ's heritage is looked after
- in the area where Pakeha culture and Maori culture first got to know each other.

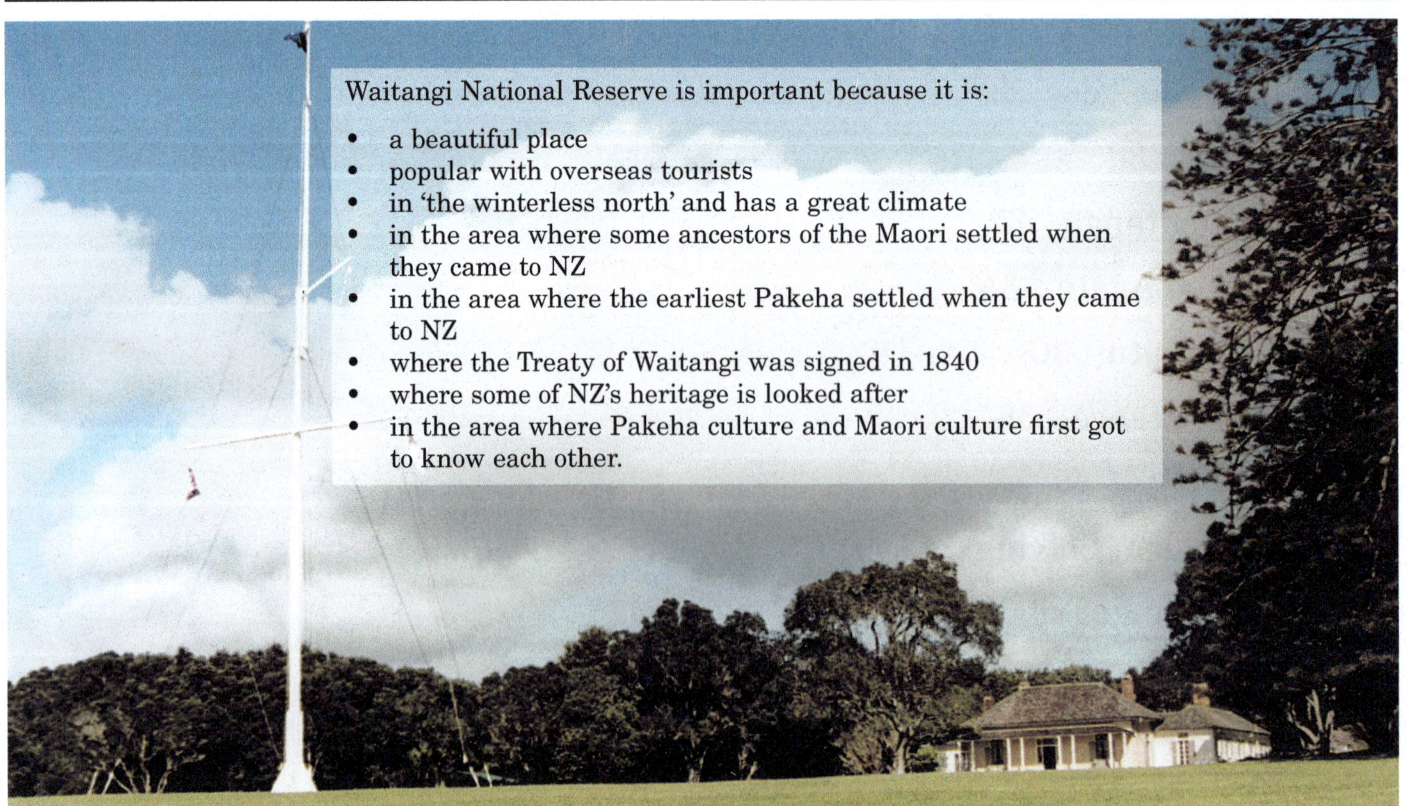

challenges

1 (a) Make a sketch of the map of the world and mark in Britain, Europe, Australia, Polynesia, and NZ.

(b) Find the answers to these three questions:

(i) If one of your ancestors was transported from Britain to Australia in 1800 for stealing a loaf of bread to feed her hungry family, what official term would have been used to describe her?

(ii) For Pakeha settlers it was a long way to come in a leaky old sailing ship. Describe the route that people would have had to use from Britain to NZ before the building of canals and aeroplanes.

(iii) Maori ancestors came from a place called Hawaiki; in what part of the world was Hawaiki?

(c) Make a sketch of the North Island of NZ and mark in Waitangi.

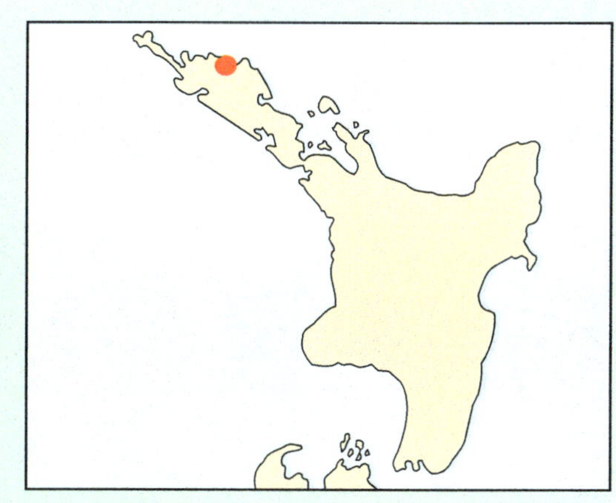

2 **Look at the map of Waitangi National Reserve:**

(a) Have you ever visited the Treaty House or seen a picture of it before?

(b) Do you live north OR south of Waitangi?

(c) What do the red lines stand for?

(d) What does the black broken line stand for?

(e) Find the name of a former Governor-General (the British Queen's representative in NZ) who has a high point named after him.

(f) What is the distance between the small town of Paihia and the Waitangi Golf Club?

(g) About how long would it take you to walk from Paihia to the Treaty House?

(h) What two routes could you take to get from Paihia to Haruru Falls?

(i) How long is the bridge over the mouth of the Waitangi River?

(j) What information does the map give you about the Waitangi River?

(k) If you drove west from Waitangi Golf Club what sort of vegetation would be on your right?

(l) Over which creek has a boardwalk been built?

(m) *Waitangi National Reserve has 506 hectares.* Which word in that sentence means a park set aside for everyone to enjoy?

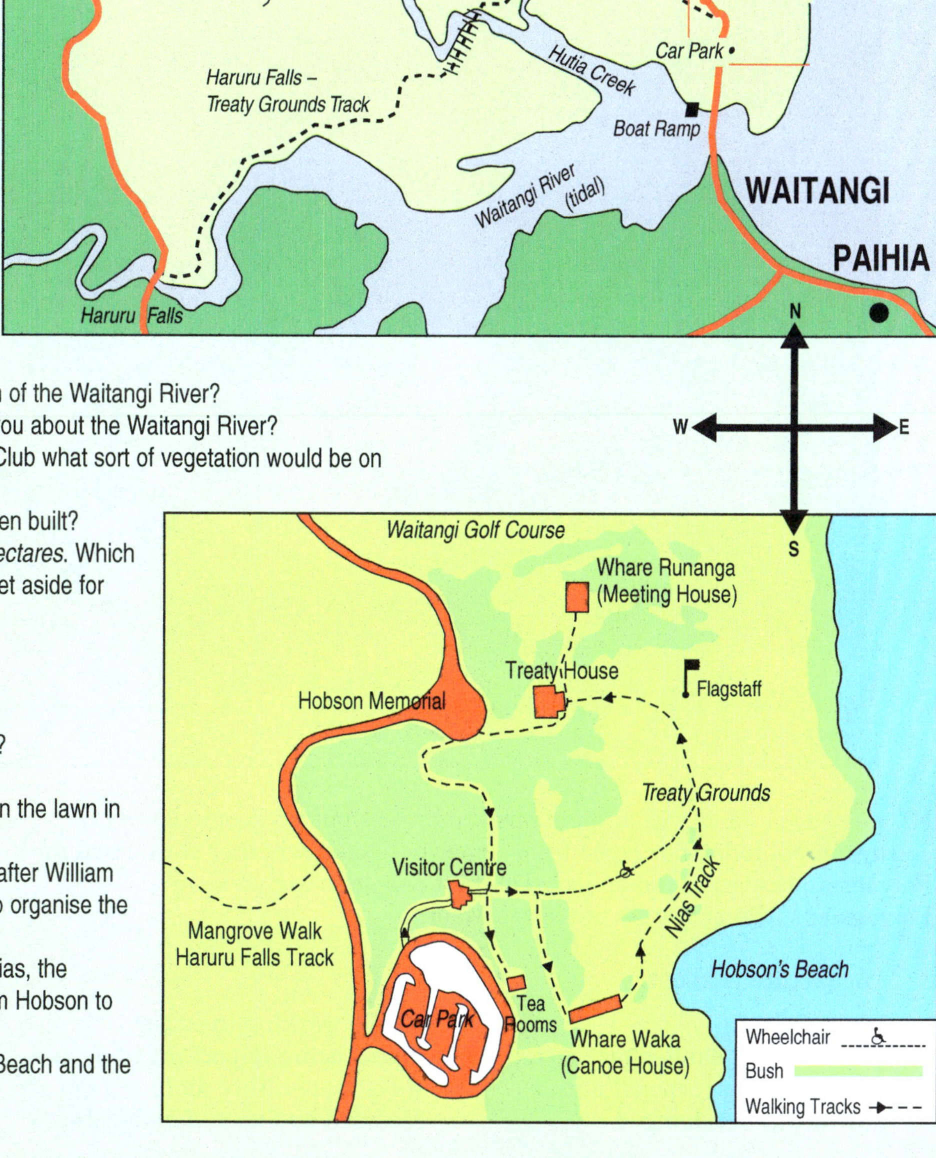

3 **Look at the map of Waitangi:**

(a) What does Whare Waka mean?

(b) What does the darker green stand for?

(c) What does Whare Runanga mean?

(d) What cultural (man-made) feature is on the lawn in front of the Treaty House?

(e) What two features have been named after William Hobson, the man sent by the British to organise the Treaty of Waitangi in 1840?

(f) What feature has been named after Nias, the captain of the ship that brought William Hobson to the bay?

(g) Which grounds lie between Hobsons Beach and the Treaty House?

2

Land

Land became important to the first settlers

The NZ bush was dark with evergreen trees and birds but no animal pests. Maori burned some bush to clear ground to grow food.

NZ was once a land with a lot of birds and trees but no people. Every culture in NZ today has come from somewhere else, whether they came in Polynesian canoes or jumbo jets. The first people to arrive were Polynesians, the ancestors of today's Maori.

The pa in the picture was at Wanganui. John Gilfillan painted it. John left NZ later, in the 1840s, after his wife and children were killed.

The picture is about:

- Maori culture
- people facing challenges
- people having responsibilities
- how work has changed
- people working together
- places being important to people
- ways that culture and heritage are recorded and passed on by others
- how features of a landscape can show people's past activities.

Maori had strong feelings for the land

- They called the country Aotearoa, land of the long white cloud.
- Land was Papatuanuku, the mother.
- Land was divided up amongst tribes.
- People were responsible for protecting the land.
- People had spiritual connections to land through their ancestors.
- Their mana was tied to land – without their land they were shamed.
- The tribe (iwi) owned land together; individuals did not own land.
- Land was their main resource (thing from which they got the means to live).
- Boundaries were natural features and boundary stones.
- Each tribe had its own warriors and war parties (taua) to defend its land.
- Places told stories of events that had happened there.
- The people belonged to the land rather than the land belonging to them.
- Ancestors were buried in special places such as caves.
- Land featured in spoken stories and histories: Maori had no written language.
- The people became tangata whenua – people of the land.

challenges

1 Look at the cartoon and point out the following things in it:

(a) the name of the cartoonist
(b) the title of the cartoon
(c) a comment by an observor in the cartoon
(d) the land of NZ
(e) how the ancestors of Maori voyaged to NZ
(f) how the earliest Pakeha would have voyaged to NZ
(g) how people coming to live nowadays arrive
(h) a cultural feature, such as a building, put on the land by early Maori
(i) a cultural feature put on the land by Pakeha.

2 Look at the pa picture on page 4:

Point out in the picture where you can see or might find these:

(a) forests that gave food, building material, medicine and art-work
(b) weapons and tools that were made from wood, stone, and bone
(c) tribal elders (kaumatua) teaching traditions and names of ancestors to children
(d) a whare wananga (house of learning)
(e) a tohunga (priest) passing on special knowledge to the best students
(f) children playing
(g) people plaiting flax to make clothes or kete
(h) a small whare that would be smoky in winter
(i) pataka on stilts used to store food
(j) palisade fence protecting the pa
(k) carving as decoration
(l) a whanau family group
(m) several whanau making a hapu subtribe
(n) people sharing work
(o) a chief (rangatira) who had mana and was tapu; some women were chiefs
(p) people learning knowledge of ancestors off by heart in the tribal whakapapa (genealogies)
(q) herbal remedies being used for illness or injuries
(r) an animal whose skin might later cover flax rain capes

3

Meetings

The meeting of cultures was an important event

Captain Cook landing in NZ in 1769. One day when Endeavour was anchored off a beach near present day Napier, a young boy called Taiata, from Tahiti, was leaning over its side as James Cook tried to barter cloth for the dried fish Maori had in their canoes. Suddenly some Maori grabbed Taiata and carried him off. 'Open fire,' ordered James. Taiata jumped into the water. Frantically he headed for the Endeavour. Sailors lowered a boat, rowed to him, and snatched him up. James Cook called the place Cape Kidnappers but was upset because he'd killed two Maori during the rescue.

Culture is a word used to describe the way a certain group of people behaves and thinks. For example in NZ, Pakeha culture and Maori culture share some ways of behaving and thinking but don't share other ways. There is no right or wrong culture, just different cultures.

Pakeha and Maori started to get to know each other in the late 18th century after the voyages of Englishman Captain James Cook to NZ.

James Cook's arrival in Aotearoa was a challenge and a crisis for Maori. They thought the ship was a great white bird or god landing among them. Warriors paddled canoes around it. To show they weren't scared, they yelled, made faces, hurled stones, tried to grab the anchor chain, and invited sailors to come ashore and be clubbed. When sailors rowed towards the shore, they seemed to be goblins with eyes in the back of their heads. A goblin's walking stick produced thunder and lightning and a shag dropped dead. The children who went on board the ship were afraid to move in case the goblins put magic on them. A goblin brought them ship's biscuit and dried beef. The chief goblin patted one of the boys on the head and gave him a nail.

James Cook's writings about NZ were published in Europe. He said:

- NZ was a wonderful place for people from Europe to settle
- the best spots for settlement were Thames Valley and Bay of Islands
- NZ had great trees and soil and the land was kind
- NZ had everything to make life comfortable for new settlers
- Maori were strong, well-built, active, warlike, artistic, and brave
- Maori did not have a king or central government like Britain did.

There may have been around 100,000 Maori in NZ at this time. Not many Maori lived in the South Island. Many lived north of Auckland around bays and river mouths such as the Bay of Islands and Hokianga. Some lived around the East Cape and along the Bay of Plenty. Some lived in the Waikato, and some around Rotorua and Taranaki.

Cook was a navigator, astronomer, surveyor, map-drawer, sailor, and leader. All six of his children died before they reached the age of 30.

What Britain was like at this time:

26.7 million people	wealthy upper classes	people united in one country under one crown
democracy and laws applying to everyone	gin parlours and workhouses	Christianity and ideas from ancient civilisations
technology, science, and architecture	transportation and ships	huge industrial cities
individuals own land and land is all important	children working, being educated, and hard winters	poor lower classes and diseases
reading and writing culture with a long written history	money and trade with other countries	horse-drawn vehicles and canals
police and courts	animals	roads and highwaymen

Captain Cook's ship Endeavour. About 100 men - crew, scientists and observers - were on board. The ship was small and uncomfortable. Cook's cabin was about 2.4m x 1.5m. The Navy wanted Cook to observe the transit of Venus across the face of the sun from Tahiti, due in 1769. After that, he was to sail south to latitude 40 in search of the southern continent and then sail west to NZ.

As a captain, Cook got a reputation for being tough but fair. He set an example by not getting involved with native women as others did. He made sailors drink spruce beer and wild celery soup to stop scurvy, a disease caused by lack of vitamin C that put bright red patches on sailors' skin and made their gums swell and bleed. James Cook had sailors who refused his cure flogged. He also had a sailor flogged for raiding a Maori kumara patch.

challenges

1 Look at the pictures:

(a) In what ways was *Endeavour* different to a Maori canoe?
(b) What do they suggest about how the nature of work has changed over time?
(c) What things about Pakeha would Maori have found strange?
(d) What things about Maori would the Pakeha have found strange?

2 Suggest a reason that James Cook:

(a) voyaged to NZ
(b) recorded his ideas about places and environments in NZ
(c) thought that NZ could be an important place for Britain
(d) had a thing about scurvy
(e) gave English names to some places in NZ.

3 Of the two groups, Pakeha and Maori, at the early time of contact, which group had:

(a) a reading and writing culture?
(b) a speaking and oral culture?
(c) individual ownership of land?
(d) communal ownership of land?

4

Resources

A resource is something people can use to get money. NZ was an important place for Pakeha to get new resources

About early sealing in NZ

- On a visit to NZ, Captain Cook ate seal meat, used seal hide to mend *Endeavour*'s rigging, and stowed away seal oil for lamps. He reported great numbers of seals on the rocks and isles near the south coast.
- NZ fur seals and sea lions were hunted for their skin; elephant seals were hunted for their oil.
- NZ seal skins were taken to Britain and China and made into felt hats.
- Sealers often lived on starvation rations unless they caught food such as goneys (young wandering albatrosses). Home was a tent or a rough flax hut, or an upturned boat. They lived among seal carcases, drying skins and smoke from cauldron fires; they spent their time skinning, sorting, pegging and drying skins. They often had to stay in a place for several years before the ship that dropped them off, returned, and all the time they lived in fear of attack by Maori.

NZ's fur seal is famous because it dives deeper and longer than any other fur seal. Seals don't hunt under a full moon because the extra light will make them more visible to the sharks and killer whales who hunt them. But they had no protection against the sealing ships that came from 1790 on from Sydney, Tasmania and Britain, and later America. Gangs slaughtered seals by tens of thousands. By the 1830s there were not enough seals left to make it worthwhile for ships to come.

About early whaling in NZ

- Almost every bit of the whale has had its uses at some time. Ambergris, for example, from the intestines of the sperm whale, was used in perfumes. Most valuable was whale oil. Whale blubber was boiled in big pots called trypots to get the oil, which was put into barrels.
- Deep-sea whalers hunted sperm whales around the world. At the end of the 18th century they began calling in to the Bay of Islands for food, water and firewood, and to give crews a rest. Several Maori served as crew on whalers and travelled the world.
- Shore (bay) whaling to hunt the right whale developed about 1820 in NZ. The whalers set up a shore-station of maybe 100 men in huts. Some married Maori women. When they sighted a whale they put out to sea in whaling boats. During the off-season they looked after their small farms or collected flax to trade with visiting Australian ships.
- Neither sealers nor whalers tried to change Maori culture.

Shore whalers hunted during the calving season because the female whales came inshore to give birth and when the whalers killed the young calves, they were able to trap the mothers who refused to leave their calves. Whaling was tough and dangerous work. Both sealing and whaling were called robber industries because they took without thinking about the future.

About the early kauri industry in NZ

- The kauri was the king of the NZ trees. It might be 30 metres up its massive trunk to its first branch.
- A kauri tree is one of the oldest living things in the world; the tree in the picture might be several hundred, even 2000 years old. It was among hundreds of thousands of hectares of kauri forest that grew from the north to about Katikati on the East Coast and Kawhia on the West Coast.
- Other countries such as Britain wanted kauri for building. The kauri industry ran from 1772 to about 1908.
- Hokianga became the second largest Pakeha settlement, after Kororareka. Its shipyard and sawmill built three large ships.

Kauri fellers taking a break.

challenges

1 Different times – different styles

This is a 21st century wish-list from a young New Zealander. Find the one thing on it which would have been available to the early sealers and whalers. They would never have been able to imagine the rest.

MP3 player	mini disc player	cellphone	jet-ski
trip to Disneyland	BMX bike	laptop	computer
Internet	car	PlayStation 2	rollerblades	go-ped
digital camera	Dickies gear	flat screen TV	Pokemon
skateboard	Harry Potter books	All Blacks jersey	
ticket to next Olympic Games	a quiet place to think		
digital watch	DVD player	Vans shoes	
martial arts course	Silver Ferns bib	digital TV	

2 Read the story below and prepare a cartoon strip about James Caddell and Tokitoki:

3 Look at the pictures of sealing, whaling and kauri felling:

(a) How many of the whaling boats are in a safe position?
(b) Why are the whaling ships standing so far off?
(c) Why would whaling ships need a constant supply of firewood?
(d) What sort of person would have made a good whaler?
(e) Why would most NZ whaling stations have been in the South Island?
(f) What different contacts would the whalers have had with Maori?
(g) How are the seals being killed?
(h) How would you describe the place that seals like to live?
(i) Why would no Maori have been living in such places?
(j) What would sealers and whalers have done for entertainment?
(k) Why are there groups today who work to stop sealing, whaling and kauri felling?
(l) What does early sealing and whaling show about how work has changed over time?
(m) What is likely to happen in the next hour after each of the 3 particular events shown?
(n) Which bits of technology would have been new to Maori?
(o) Which one shows an activity that would change the look of the land?

James Caddell was 16 years old when he arrived at Stewart Island as a sealer in 1810. With five sailors, he set off in a sealing boat for the island. They landed and immediately a party of Maori attacked them. The Maori killed the five men. But Tokitoki, the chief's niece, claimed the life of James by throwing a cloak over him. James married Tokitoki. He got tattooed. He was a good fighter and this, with his marriage, gave him the mana of a chief.

5

Changes

The movement of people can change places and people

barter = to swap goods

A famous trader in NZ was Philip Tapsell from Denmark. At the invitation of Te Arawa chiefs of Rotorua, he settled at Maketu in Bay of Plenty in 1830. He became the agent for a Sydney trading firm and in exchange for flax supplied goods such as muskets and gunpowder to Maori.

Some traders had Maori wives – Philip Tapsell married Karuhi, a sister of a Ngapuhi chief. But traders did not try to change Maori society.

The Pakeha bartering over a pig and a coil of flax is Joel Polack from Britain, a trader at Kororareka (today's Russell) in the Bay of Islands. His bitter enemy was Benjamin Turner, who owned a grog-shop and had a reputation as a land-shark. Joel and Benjamin had a gun battle on the Kororareka beach in 1837 and Joel wounded Benjamin. Seven years later they had another duel and wounded each other.

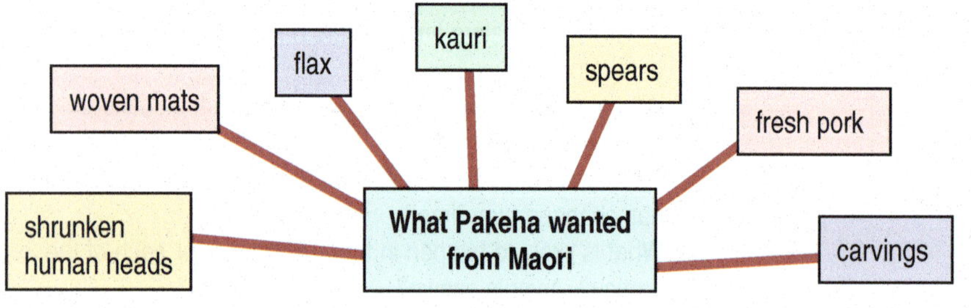

Example: 25 bags of potatoes would buy a musket. One ton of scraped flax would buy one or two muskets.

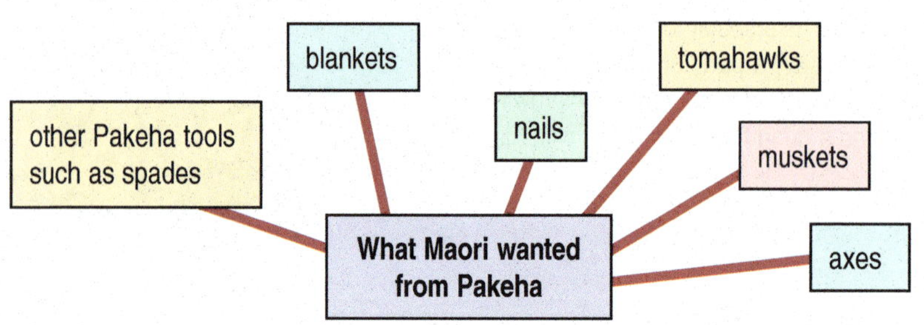

A stone cross at Oihi Bay in the Bay of Islands is a memorial to Samuel Marsden's first sermon in New Zealand.
Samuel Marsden, chaplain to the New South Wales convict station, arrived in the Bay of Islands in 1814 and set up the Anglican Church Missionary Society. The missionary ship brought horses and cattle, which amazed the Maori. At Oihi Bay, a young chief called Ruatara gathered people on Christmas morning and interpreted Marsden's sermon from the text: 'Behold, I bring you glad tidings of great joy.'

The missionaries tried to stop some Maori ways of doing things such as:
- polygamy (chiefs having more than one wife)
- cannibalism (eating of human flesh)
- slavery.

Missionary scandals included:
- a missionary getting too friendly with Maori females
- missionaries trading in muskets
- some missionaries buying lots of land from Maori.

Missionaries were useful to Maori because they:
- traded Pakeha goods and introduced the tomahawk
- taught farming skills such as how to use the horse and plough
- taught how to use Pakeha tools such as spades instead of ko (Maori digging tool)
- taught reading and writing
- acted as peacemakers in the musket wars between Maori tribes of the late 1820s and early 1830s
- knew how to dig out musket balls from Maori warriors in terrible pain from their injuries
- became friends with chiefs and took some overseas
- believed in wine as a tonic.

Scenes such as this can happen when two cultures clash. The Maori are threatening to destroy the potato crop belonging to Henry and William Williams, who had a mission station at Paihia. Missionaries didn't live with Maori as some traders did but they tried to get them to become Christians. A mission station usually had a house, farm, orchard, schoolroom and chapel. Sometimes it had sleeping quarters for Maori children and adults being taught or trained as teachers. A printer called William Colenso set up a printing press to print Bibles at the Paihia mission.

At the time Pakeha thought missionaries were doing Maori a big favour. Today the thinking is that while missionaries brought Christianity and technology, they also tried to make Maori culture more like British culture, bought a lot of land from Maori, and in the early days traded in muskets.

challenges

1 Look at the trade items on page 10.
Which trade item/s:
(a) came from the pigs that Pakeha introduced into NZ?
(b) would have been used to make rope?
(c) would have been used to make spars for masts and booms of ships?
(d) was a food similar to kumara and planted by Captain Cook in NZ?
(e) could be called a Maori artefact (something made by people)?

2 Look at the pictures about Pakeha and Maori cultures meeting.
Which one/s show/s:
(a) two cultures meeting in peace?
(b) two cultures in conflict?
(c) one culture using a resource in a way that the other culture had not used it?
(d) two cultures in a trading situation?
(e) a group who tried to change ways of doing things in another culture?
(f) a group whose actions are seen differently to how they were seen at the time?
(g) a group who helped bring the idea of farms to NZ?

3 Work with a mate on this problem-solving.
Work out the main obvious problem, any underlying problems, possible solutions, possible results of the solutions, the best solution.

It is 1820 in the Bay of Islands and you are a Maori chief. The missionaries you have been protecting are starting to refuse to trade with you in the muskets you desperately want; and a Pakeha trader in your area has been trying to cheat the tribe and has broken tapu by going onto a kumara plot.

4 Draw a picture to illustrate an event from this story:

Early Pakeha in NZ had exciting lives. Marianne Williams, missionary wife, had eleven children. One day in January 1824 a chief called Tohitapu, who lived about 3 km away from the Williams family at Paihia, jumped over the Williams' fence and hurt his foot. Waving his mere, he demanded utu for his sore foot, and threatened to burn the house down and have a gun battle. Marianne lived through two nights and a day of terror until things calmed down, and her husband gave Tohitapu a pot the chief wanted.

6

New Technology

New technology and ideas brought changes to culture

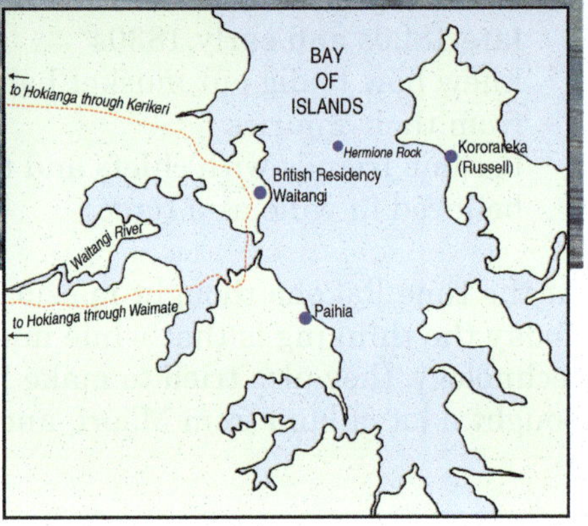

BAY OF ISLANDS
to Hokianga through Kerikeri
Hermione Rock
Kororareka (Russell)
British Residency Waitangi
Waitangi River
to Hokianga through Waimate
Paihia

Watering Bay, painted here in 1838, was at the northern end of Kororareka. A spring gave fresh water to sailors, who used the beaches to repair and refit ships because the water was deep close inshore. Sailors made tents out of sails. Maori brought potatoes and pork to trade with sailors.

Kororareka (given the English name of Russell in 1840) means 'Sweet penguin'. Legend says an old chief lay dying and asked for penguin to eat. One was found. The chief was too weak to eat but he drank some water in which it had boiled. 'Ka reka te korora,' he murmured ('How sweet is the penguin').

Kororareka was the biggest Pakeha settlement in NZ before 1840. The narrow hilly peninsula protected ships at anchor and it was close to the kauri being felled and taken overseas. The beach was the only street. Town was a line of raupo whares and a few timber houses. Some runaway convicts hid there and the many grog shops (raupo whares with barrels of rum from Port Jackson on trestles) were open all hours. Missionaries called it 'the hell-hole of the Pacific'. When a group of citizens formed an association to get law and order, one of the rules was that every member had to have a good musket, a bayonet, a brace of pistols, a cutlass and at least sixty rounds of ball cartridge.

Pakeha needed chiefs for protection, and the chiefs wanted Pakeha trade goods and skills. One famous Ngapuhi chief in the Bay of Islands was Hongi Hika (1772–1828). He protected the missionaries, knowing it would bring Pakeha with tools and weapons to trade. A great warrior, he led war parties down to the East Cape and brought back prisoners and preserved heads.

In 1820 he went to England with missionary Thomas Kendall and another chief, Waikato. There he met the King and people gave Hongi Hika presents such as a suit of chain mail. On the way home they stopped in Sydney; Hongi sold most of his presents and bought 300 muskets. This started an arms race back in NZ because other Bay of Islands hapu had to get muskets in self-defence. Hongi marched off to deal with his enemies down south.

Hongi was said to be gentle and polite, and especially kind to his blind senior wife whose advice he listened to. When his eldest son was killed in battle, he was very upset. He was wounded himself in a January 1827 battle but lingered until March of the next year. His place of burial was kept top secret.

In the early 19th century, especially during the 1820s, Maori tribes fought other Maori tribes in raids and battles in places around the top of the South Island and in places around most of the North Island. Nobody knows exactly how many thousands and thousands of Maori were killed by other Maori in these inter-tribal wars but historians describe the wars as 'blood-thirsty' and 'slaughter'.

Hongi Hika, famous chief.

How contact with Pakeha affected Maori:

Maori were no longer isolated from Europe.

Muskets changed old ways of fighting because a tutua, a nobody, could hide behind a tree and kill a great chief.

Muskets caused shifts of Maori population as people fled the fighting. E.g. Te Rauparaha went south with his Ngati Toa tribe from Kawhia down the west coast of the North Island to Kapiti Island. Then he invaded South Island tribes.

Maori had no immunity to Pakeha diseases such as flu and thousands died.

Maori learned about different political systems such as the British Crown and parliament.

The fighting that caused thousands of Maori to move to different areas to live made later land claims very complicated.

Some Maori travelled to other places such as Britain, North America, Australia.

Some tribes that had contact with missionaries became Christians.

Maori learned to read and write.

Maori were introduced to and liked Pakeha technology.

Maori learned about money, trade and markets.

Maori learned to grow new crops such as potatoes, wheat, maize.

Children were born to Maori mothers and Pakeha fathers.

Maori learned to cook and sew.

Some Maori shifted to unhealthy flax swamps to get flax for traders.

Maori replaced many of their tools with Pakeha ones.

Cannibalism stopped.

Maori adopted some Pakeha technology instead of their own – e.g. the British longboat was better for transport than the canoe and so Maori made only carved ceremonial canoes.

Musket wars between the tribes killed thousands.

Slavery stopped.

Maori saw Pakeha break tapu and go unpunished.

Examples of Pakeha technology

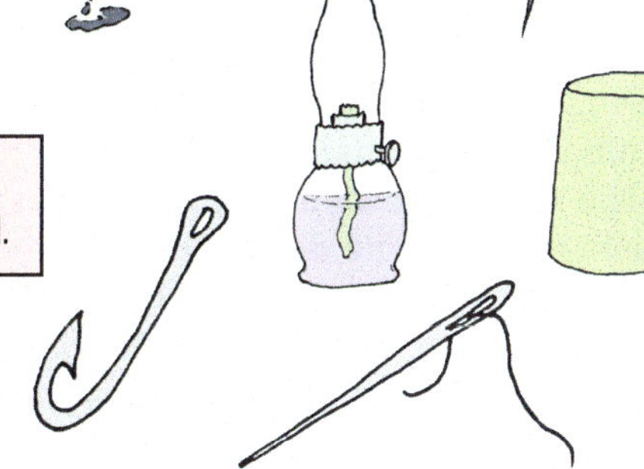

challenges

1 Look at the map and picture of Kororareka:

(a) What is the modern name for Kororareka?
(b) What is the name of the rock between Kororareka and Waitangi?
(c) Which two different routes to the Hokianga does the map show?
(d) Does the map or the picture best show how sheltered Kororareka was for boats and ships?
(e) How would Watering Bay have got its name?
(f) What are the Pakeha sailors doing and what might be in the barrels?
(g) Where might the Maori canoe be going?
(h) What reasons would Maori have had for thinking Kororareka was important?
(i) What reasons would Pakeha have had for thinking Kororareka was important?
(j) What did the missionaries at Paihia think of it?

2 Look at the picture of Hongi Hika and prepare a three-sentence talk on it to share with the class.

3 Look at how contact with Pakeha affected Maori. Find something that shows or is about:

(a) a social challenge or crisis to Maori
(b) a technological challenge or crisis to Maori
(c) an economic challenge or crisis to Maori
(d) a political challenge or crisis to Maori
(e) a cultural challenge or crisis to Maori
(f) a technological change that helped change Maori culture
(g) a technological change that exposed Maori culture to new ideas
(h) a result for Maori culture of such exposure to new ideas
(i) how technological change affected the way Maori kept and passed on their heritage.

4 Cultural contact between Pakeha and Maori was an important event that they both experienced over time. Make up a poster or cartoon strip to show this. Try to show: the cause of the event; the groups involved; how the event affected people's lives in different ways; how different groups experienced the same event differently.

7

Justice

An early ask for social justice

Captain Stewart gets into trouble

In 1830 Captain Stewart of the ship *Elizabeth* was in NZ waters making a deal. For a cargo of 50 tons of flax, he would take Te Rauparaha, leader of Ngati Toa at Kapiti Island, and a war party of about 100 warriors, from Kapiti to Akaroa. Te Rauparaha had unfinished business with his enemy Tamaiharanui of Ngai Tahu down there.

The ship sailed to Akaroa and anchored in the harbour. The 100 warriors hid on board. Captain Stewart sent messages to Tamaiharanui that a ship had arrived to trade guns for flax. Tamaiharanui came aboard with his wife and 11-year-old daughter Nga Roimata. Te Rauparaha and his warriors leaped out of their hiding places and captured Tamaiharanui. They went ashore and burned and sacked his village, killing all the people they could find.

The *Elizabeth* sailed back to Kapiti with 50 prisoners including Tamaiharanui and his wife and daughter. There are several versions of what happened on this voyage. One says that Tamaiharanui strangled his daughter and threw her into the sea so she would escape slavery. Another version says his wife dived overboard.

Captain Stewart reached Kapiti and kept Tamaiharanui on board for another five weeks until he gave up hope of getting any more flax from Ngati Toa. He handed Tamaiharanui over to Ngati Toa. Most versions agree the wives of Ngati Toa chiefs tortured Tamaiharanui to death.

There was no British court in NZ. Pakeha who committed crimes in NZ could be charged in New South Wales but when Captain Stewart was charged in a Sydney court with helping Te Rauparaha, all the witnesses had gone and so that was the end of the case.

Te Rauparaha and Tamaiharanui had acted how Maori expected them to act. But a Pakeha had got involved. Events such as this and the general lawlessness of Pakeha in NZ made Maori chiefs worry.

In 1831, 13 northern chiefs met at Kerikeri and signed a petition to send to Britain. A petition is a request written on paper and presented to someone in authority. This was an early ask for social justice.

The petition said to Britain:

- you be our friend and guardian
- save us from foreign threat (many French and American ships visited NZ)
- save us from the teasing of other tribes
- save us from the bad behaviour of British people who live in and visit NZ.

Why the chiefs chose Britain to send a petition to:

- most Pakeha in NZ were British
- Maori had a strong idea of a close relationship with Britain
- some chiefs had gone to England and some had met the King
- missionaries talked of how the British Crown had a fatherly and motherly interest in Maori
- the British Crown had given chiefs presents like swords
- Maori were keen to learn about the Royal Family and their kainga (village) in London
- Maori traditions talked about the British being the first Europeans to come to NZ
- Maori were impressed with British ships and British power.

Results of the petition:

When they got the petition, the British chose one man, James Busby, to be their representative in NZ. He was called the British Resident.

On 17 May 1833 James went ashore at Paihia where missionary Henry Williams lived. While their house was being built at Waitangi, James and his wife Agnes were to stay with the Williams and Henry was to fill James in on what had been happening in NZ. James was 33 years old and he had a tough job ahead. It didn't pay well. He did get a uniform and the frame of a house to bring to NZ but no land to build the house on.

James told the chiefs and people he was there to:

- catch escaped convicts from Australia and send them back
- protect Pakeha and Maori in NZ
- protect British trade with NZ
- set up British influence
- calm the jealous and divided chiefs
- encourage chiefs to keep law and order
- deal with the bad treatment of crews by ship captains
- deal with other crimes such as stealing, murder, assault and arguments over land boundaries.

Poor James:

- He and his boss – Richard Bourke, Governor of New South Wales – did not always get on well.
- It took months for letters to go between NZ and Australia so to get permission to do things was going to take for ever.
- He was going to have to spend a lot of his poor salary on presents for the chiefs.
- He was nicknamed 'man-o-war without guns'; man-o-war was a war ship. When Maori raided his own house he had no power to do anything.
- Today it is seen that James did the best he could. He was a one-man band; he had no police, no soldiers and no warship.

James Busby built this house at Waitangi in 1834. It stood on a small rise that had amazing views of the ocean and looked down on Paihia. Today it is called the Treaty House because this is where the treaty was signed. James brought in several hundred sheep and two bullocks; he made a vineyard, big vegetable gardens and a forest nursery.

James lost his job in 1840 with the signing of the Treaty of Waitangi because NZ no longer needed a British Resident. He kept his house but during a war in the Bay of Islands between some Maori chiefs and British soldiers, the house was wrecked. James fixed it up but after he left NZ in 1871 sheep camped in it and shearers used the front of it to shear in. In 1932 Governor-General Lord Bledisloe bought the house and grounds and gave it to the people of NZ.

challenges

1 To which person or group would the following comments be referring?

(a) *'Bit rude earning a buck by getting mixed up in a feud between a couple of chiefs.'*
(b) *'What a hassle, trying to get them brought to justice if you had to take them all the way to Aussie.'*
(c) *'Poor kid must have been terrified out of her skull.'*
(d) *'Bet he was wild with himself for trusting that cunning chief.'*
(e) *'He had no show of doing his job properly because the British government didn't give him resources.'*
(f) *'Probably pumped to get the guy out of his hair and settled in a job miles away in NZ.'*
(g) *'So that's where the famous rugby cup got its name.'*

2 From this chapter find:

(a) a place with an important history
(b) a place that is important to Pakeha and Maori
(c) a place that shows people's past activities
(d) a man-made feature that has survived for over 160 years
(e) a job that no longer exists in NZ
(f) a way government tried to help get social justice for a group of people
(g) an important event for Maori
(h) an important event for Pakeha
(i) an important event for both Pakeha and Maori
(j) an event that influenced relationships between Pakeha and Maori
(k) a difference between the British and Maori political systems
(l) a decision by the British government that would affect people's lives
(m) a reason that the Maori chiefs sent a petition to Britain
(n) a reason the British government sent James Busby to NZ
(o) an example of how James Busby kept his own culture when he moved to NZ
(p) an example of British culture being set up in NZ
(q) a group whose actions shaped the lives and experiences of others
(r) an individual whose actions shaped the lives and experiences of others
(s) what people at the time thought of James Busby
(t) what people today think of James Busby.

8

Events

Important events for communities, cultures, and nation

The Waitangi area had wonderful scenery and resources. This is how an artist saw a piece of it around the time that James Busby arrived.

Scene

20 March 1834. Big tent on Busby's new lawn at Waitangi. Three flags on short poles in front of the tent. Bay of Islands VIPs in best dress – Pakeha settlers and missionaries, about 25 Maori chiefs. James Busby. Men in naval uniforms. British and American ships in harbour including British man-of-war HMS *Alligator*.

What happened

James explained why he'd invited everyone. The ship *Sir George Murray* was built at the Hokianga and launched in 1830. Three years later it sailed into Sydney and the authorities seized it because it had no national flag. To make matters worse, there were two Maori chiefs on board. To protect NZ ships and get cargo into foreign ports duty free, NZ needed a national flag so that ships built in NZ could register under it. A national flag would also be a step towards settled government.

The chiefs from the Bay of Islands and Hokianga were to choose which flag they wanted. Henry Williams had drawn three designs and the designs had been made up in Sydney into proper flags which the *Alligator* had just brought back.

The chiefs voted for the flag the Anglican missionaries already used. It was run up the main flagpole on the lawn alongside the British flag. HMS *Alligator* gave a 21-gun salute. This flag was known as the flag of the United Tribes of NZ, and is the one Ko Huiarau, the United Tribes, still use today. The Union Jack replaced it in 1840 as the official flag.

James could now arrange for NZ-built ships to be registered in the name of the Independent Tribes of NZ. The British King recognised it as the national flag of NZ. This was a sign to Maori that the British Crown recognised their mana and the mana of NZ.

1834 flag.

Present flag.

The rescue of Betty Guard

Another event that made the British government anxious about NZ was the Betty Guard incident. Betty was 16 when she married Jacky Guard, ex-convict and 23 years older than her. Jacky set up the first shore whaling station in NZ, at Te Awaiti Tory Channel. In 1834 he took Betty and their two young children, John and Louisa, to visit Sydney. They got shipwrecked off Cape Egmont but they all survived, and the crew used the ship's sails to make tents.

Maori attacked them. Betty was lucky. Twice a tomahawk struck her head; twice the large comb in her hair saved her. She and Jacky, John and Louisa, and the surviving crew were captured. Jacky and others were sent to Port Nicholson at Wellington to get a cask of gunpowder for the Maori who held Betty and the children as ransom. But the wind blew Jacky off course and they had to go to Sydney.

The man-o-war *Alligator* and another ship were sent to Taranaki to rescue Betty and the children. They found them at a pa, and attacked and burnt the pa. The Maori fled with their prisoners to another pa. Betty and Louisa were swapped for a captured chief. The vessels turned their firepower on the Maori pa for three hours. A party landed and a chief with John on his back staggered on to the beach. A sailor snatched the boy; another shot the chief.

The rescue wrecked two pa – Te Namu and Waimate. Louisa died eight months later. People in England criticised the violence against Maori.

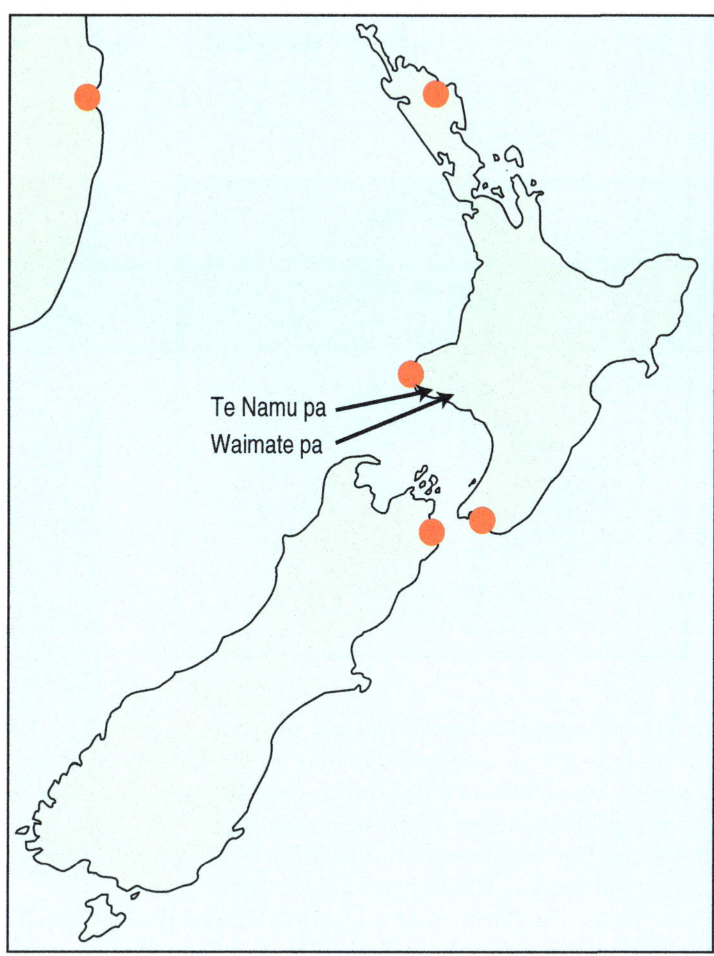

challenges

1 Look at the 1834 flag:

(a) A red cross on a white background is the St George's cross (St George is the patron saint of England). Where is the St George's cross on this flag?
(b) What other colours are on the flag?
(c) What would the stars and the colour blue stand for?
(d) In what ways is this flag the same as the present NZ flag?
(e) In what ways is this flag different to the present NZ flag?
(f) Why would the flag have made the captain and crew of *Sir George Murray* happy?
(g) What events showed that the flag's mana was recognised officially?

2 The new flag:

(a) What sort of challenge did James Busby face over the *Sir George Murray* affair?
(b) What different groups did he get to help him sort out a solution?
(c) Why could the choosing of a flag be called a step towards NZ getting its own identity?
(d) Why would the flag event have been important to the Maori chiefs?
(e) Why would the flag event have been important to the British?
(f) How would the flag event have influenced relationships between Maori chiefs and the British?

3 The rescue of Betty Guard:

(a) Name a challenge that Jacky Guard faced.
(b) Name a group trained to help Jacky Guard.
(c) Why would the places where the Betty Guard rescue took place have become important to both Pakeha and Maori?
(d) For which individual Pakeha and Maori would the places where the rescue took place have become important?
(e) How would the rescue have influenced the relationship between Maori and British?
(f) Pick a time when someone (give the name) in the story would have felt
(i) relieved (ii) sad (iii) safe (iv) terrified
(v) angry (vi) grateful (vii) cold (viii) disappointed

4 Look at the map. Each dot shows where one of the places in the box is found. Make your own copy of the map and put where each place is.

Paihia, Cape Egmont, Port Nicholson, Tory Channel, Sydney

Social Organisation

Social organisation in the Bay of Islands

Baron Charles de Thierry.

Hongi Hika with Kendall and Waikato in England; Hongi is on the left.

When Hongi Hika and Waikato were in London with missionary Thomas Kendall, they met a Frenchman called Baron de Thierry, who talked to them about buying land in NZ, although it was to be Tamati Waka Nene who granted land to the baron in Hokianga.

Later the baron sent a letter to James Busby from Tahiti. He said he was the Sovereign Chief of NZ, and he would be coming 'with armed ships, with guns, and with property' to set up a 'sovereign and independent state' on the 4000 acres of Hokianga land that he had bought. Rumours flew round the Bay of Islands that a mad Frenchie was on the way to make NZ a French colony.

James Busby called a meeting at Waitangi on 28 October 1835. He had a document called the Declaration of Independence. Independence means you are not ruled or controlled by another. The missionaries translated it into Maori. Thirty-four northern chiefs from the North Cape to Thames, four English witnesses, and Busby, signed it.

The Declaration of the Independence of NZ (Te Whakaputanga o te Rangatiratanga o Nui Tireni) said the chiefs:

1. declared the independence of their country
2. had sovereign power and authority (were the bosses)
3. would meet at Waitangi each year to make laws, keep peace, and deal with trade; they invited the southern tribes to join them
4. agreed to send a copy of the Declaration to the King of England, to thank him for acknowledging their flag, and in return for his friendship and protection begged him to continue to be the parent of their infant state and become its Protector.

That's just a summary. It didn't use simple language like that. Instead it used legal language like this (taken from its second clause):

> 'All sovereign power and authority within the territories of the United Tribes of New Zealand is hereby declared to reside entirely and exclusively in the hereditary chiefs and heads of tribes in their collective capacity, who also declare that they will not permit any legislative authority separate from themselves in their collective capacity to exist, nor any function of government to be exercised within the said territories, unless by persons appointed by them, and acting under the authority of laws regularly enacted by them in Congress assembled.'

Tamati Waka Nene, who granted land to the mad French baron, remained a supporter of the British. When he died in 1871 the Governor of NZ wrote to London that Tamati was the Maori leader who 'did more than any other ... to establish the Queen's authority and promote colonization.'

Results of the Declaration:

- James Busby wrote to Baron de Thierry telling him to back off
- James went on collecting signatures; by 1839 52 chiefs had signed it
- the yearly meetings did not happen
- the chiefs saw it as a guarantee of their independence
- Britain agreed to recognise the country's independence and to give it its protection.

What the Declaration showed:

- NZ was a Maori country. Pakeha, including the British Resident, needed tribal protection to survive.
- if Britain ever wanted to have NZ as a colony it would have to make a treaty with NZ.

In the early 1800s people from Britain were making a mark on the land with their buildings. Here are some that have survived in the Bay of Islands.

The Kemp House in Kerikeri was built for James Kemp, who came as a missionary in 1819. It is the oldest wooden building in NZ.

Waimate North Mission House, built in 1832 for the missionaries, is the second oldest wooden building in NZ.

Christ Church in Russell, NZ's first church, was built in 1835/36. In its churchyard are the graves of Tamati Waka Nene and Hannah King Lethbridge, one of the first white women born in NZ.

The Stone Store at Kerikeri was built in 1833 as a store for the mission. A later churchman lived at Waimate but kept his library in the Stone Store, a ten-mile walk away.

challenges

1 Look at the pictures of people. Choose one to think about. Share your thoughts on it with the class.

2 The Declaration of Independence:

(a) If a comment on your school report says you show independence, what does it mean?
(b) Name some things you can make a declaration about.
(c) What kind of challenge was the baron to NZ?
(d) Which two groups in NZ met this challenge?
(e) How did the Declaration of Independence show groups and individuals working together to deal with the challenge?
(f) Where did the chiefs who signed the Declaration in 1835 come from?
(g) How many chiefs had signed it by 1839?
(h) How do you say Declaration of the Independence of NZ in Maori?
(i) Why would the chiefs have picked autumn as the time of year to meet at Waitangi each year?
(j) Suggest a reason the chiefs did not meet as planned.
(k) What two things did the tribes want from the British King?
(l) Give a reason for the Declaration of Independence.
(m) Give a result of the Declaration of Independence.

3 Look at the second clause of the Declaration. Find the meanings of the underlined words and phrases in this box:

• land	• law making	• passed on
• complete authority	• totally	
• meeting	• chiefs working together	

4 Look at the pictures of famous buildings:

(a) Give a reason that the Bay of Islands is called 'The cradle of NZ'.
(b) What do the pictures show about how knowledge of the past is handed down?
(c) Why do people today think these places are important and worth looking after?
(d) Why might these places be important to individual people today?
(e) Try making your own sketches of the historical places.

10

Pakeha Settlement

A person, an event, and the movement of people had big impacts on NZ

As a boy, Englishman Edward Gibbon Wakefield (1796–1862) was always in trouble at school. When he was 20, he raced off with a 16-year-old girl who had a rich father, and married her secretly. They had two children before she died. Four years later Edward heard of a 15-year-old schoolgirl with a rich father. He had never met her but got her out of school by sending her a note saying her mother was at death's door. Then he told her that her father had terrible money troubles and the only way to save him was for her to marry Edward. They dashed to Gretna Green in Scotland where marriage rules were not as strict as in England. Her family chased them to France and Edward got three years in Newgate prison.

He used the time in prison to work out his next money-making scheme – colonisation. As he thought the British were soon going to take over NZ, he used NZ to try out his idea.

Edward's idea was to buy land cheaply from Maori and sell it at a higher price to people from Britain.

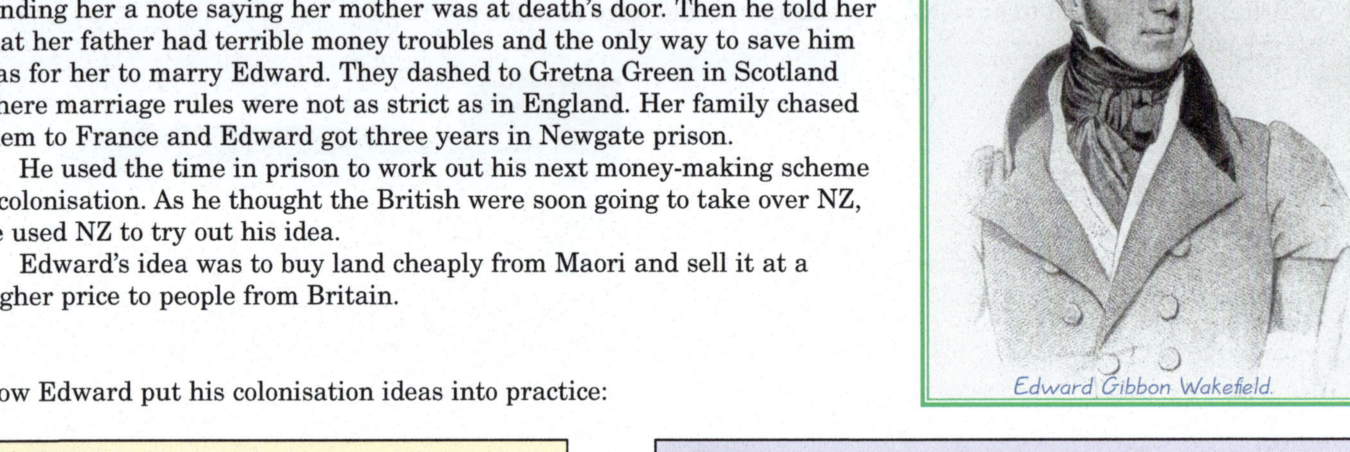

Edward Gibbon Wakefield.

How Edward put his colonisation ideas into practice:

STEP 1

Out of prison, Edward formed the New Zealand Company with headquarters in London. Rich people came to buy land in NZ that the company offered for sale even though none of them had seen it. Nor had Edward. All he knew was that it would be in the Wellington area because he thought Wellington, named after the Duke of Wellington, would be the capital of NZ.

STEP 2

He sent his only son Edward Jerningham Wakefield, with his brother Colonel William Wakefield, to scout for land in NZ. But rumours flew all over London that the government was going to take over NZ. Edward didn't want the government in charge of buying land that *he* wanted to buy cheaply. So he sent off the ship *Tory* with land buyers and surveyors and another brother, Arthur, to buy land in Wellington. The *Tory* took muskets and powder, tools, clothes, and other goods to pay for the land bought from Maori.

STEP 3

Edward sent out publicity agents to towns and villages in England and Scotland. They got several thousand people interested in moving to NZ. Edward couldn't risk them changing their minds so he decided to send them off before he'd heard how the land buying was getting on in NZ. The people gathered at London with their luggage. Rich cabin passengers brought furniture. Poorer steerage passengers crowded into the ships' holds. They were given a mattress, pillow and cooking pot. They had to provide their own bedding, knives, forks, plates, spoons and mug. Each family had to have a linen bag of spare clothes for a month. Steerage had no port holes and the only light was from open hatches battened down in storms. A family of parents and four children would sleep in an enclosure measuring 1.8 metres by 2.4 metres. The first ships left England on 3 September 1839 for NZ. This was the beginning of Pakeha going in organised groups to live in NZ. The voyage was dangerous. Sailors sprinkled the floors and decks with chloride of lime to try to control diseases. But many children died. On one voyage the steward who was responsible for getting everyone out of the hold before he fumigated, accidentally left a man down there. The man died and his young son was left an orphan. The captain promised the angry passengers he would take care of the boy but didn't.

On 22 January 1840 the first passenger ship entered the narrow heads of the harbour at Wellington.

The settlers found wind, sand, thick bush and swamps. They and their belongings were dumped on the beach to wait for surveyors to mark out streets and sections.

The settlers faced earthquakes, gales and fires. They had to learn new skills – how to build a raupo hut, how to fish, how to hunt wild pigs and birds, how to recognise danger such as tutu berries which could kill them, how to make tea from leaves of manuka, how to get through bush with no roads, how to cut down the forest with axes and crosscut saws, how to cope with being so isolated, how to make clothes, how to cope with medical emergencies and the death of children. The only way to reach the Bay of Islands was by ship and even a ship might not make it because the coasts were so dangerous and the winds so bad.

Yet by the time of the first Anniversary Day of 22 January 1841, almost 2500 people were living in Wellington.

> Chief Te Wharepouri, Atiawa chief at Petone, told Colonel William Wakefield of the New Zealand Company when more shiploads of settlers arrived: 'I thought you would have nine or ten Pakeha. I thought that I should get one placed at every pa as a white man to barter with the people and keep us supplied with arms and clothing, and that I should be able to keep these white men under my hand and regulate their trade myself.'

challenges

1 Read about Edward Wakefield and look at his picture:

(a) What might have been some of his strengths or good points?

(b) How did he and the NZ Company shape the lives and experiences of others?

(c) What was his attitude to land?

(d) How was his attitude different to that of Maori?

2 Look at the picture 'Taking leave of old England' on page 20:

(a) How suitable are the clothes for an ocean voyage of four to five months?

(b) How might the people be feeling?

(c) What challenges face these people in the next year?

(d) How might the move to NZ affect these people?

(e) How might the experiences of the wealthy people who came to NZ be different to the experiences of the poorer people?

(f) How might these people have affected NZ when they arrived?

3 Look at the picture of the arrival of the settlers on page 21:

(a) Which ship would have been the first to get to NZ?

(b) The Pakeha in the canoe is Colonel William Wakefield. What relation was he to Edward?

(c) What is William holding in his hand and why?

(d) Why was William in NZ before the settlers arrived?

4 Agents in Britain trying to convince people to move to NZ had not been to NZ so they had to use their imaginations. The soil is so fertile you just need to tickle it and you'll grow cabbages big enough to shelter you from the rain, they said. The climate is so wonderful you won't need fireplaces in your houses. Design an advertisement that the NZ Company could have used.

5 Make your own copy of this diagram and fill it out.

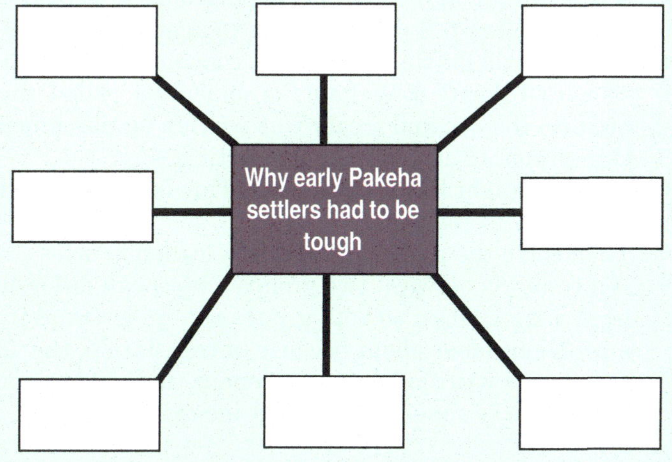

11

The Treaty

A government decision that is still affecting people's lives

When?

By 1840 Britain had decided it needed to sign a treaty with Maori chiefs

Why?

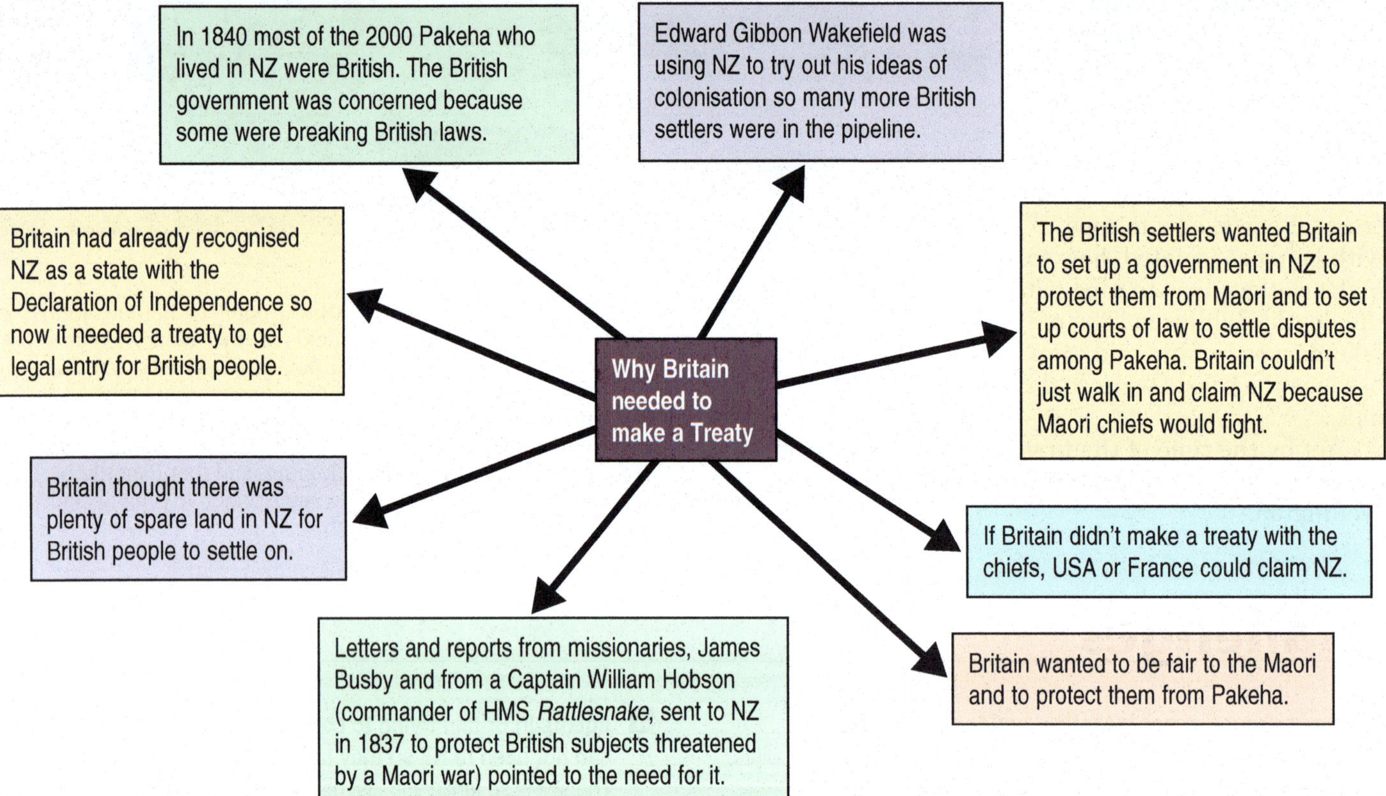

What?

- A treaty is an agreement between groups of people or countries.
- Treaties often talk about *parties* instead of people or countries.
- Other words for treaty are pact, contract, charter, covenant.
- The 1840 Treaty of Waitangi is sometimes called 'the parchment' because the original treaty was written on parchment, which is animal skin prepared as a surface for writing.
- A treaty might have a preamble. This is an introduction, saying what the treaty is about.
- Then come the points of the treaty, called articles.
- If a treaty is between two groups who speak different languages, it will need a translation so both groups can understand it. A law says that if a problem comes about because of translation, the version to use is the one that is written in the indigenous (native) language of the country where it was signed. In NZ that means Maori.

Where?

The British government sent William Hobson of the British Royal Navy to Waitangi to persuade the chiefs to recognise Queen Victoria's authority so Britain could govern NZ. He was not allowed to bribe or force the Maori. The treaty was to be signed at Waitangi because the British Resident lived there.

Who?

Captain William Hobson.

Captain William Hobson (1792–1842) left Plymouth in England, sailed to Port Jackson in Australia, and arrived in Waitangi on the HMS *Herald* on 29 January 1840. He lived on the ship but did not get on well with its captain, Joseph Nias. William had been in the navy since he was ten years old. He was slim, of medium height, smart, a Christian and a good host and speaker. He thought NZ should never be turned into a convict colony. He tried to be fair but could be stubborn. He looked older than he was because he had caught yellow fever in the tropics. When he first met the chiefs at Waitangi, an old chief pushed his way through the crowd and exclaimed: 'Alas, an old man! He will soon be dead.'

A few weeks later, William, who was now Governor of NZ, had a stroke and went to recover at the mission stations at Waimate and Paihia. From there he went to Okiato, still in the Bay of Islands and the place he made the capital of NZ for a while; later in 1840 he moved to Auckland, which he made the capital and next year shifted into the new Government House.

After William died in 1842, a chief wrote to Queen Victoria: 'Let not the new Governor be a boy or one puffed up: let not a troubler come amongst us: let him be a good man like this Governor who has just died.'

William's immediate problems

- He did not speak Maori.
- He had no legal training.
- He had no lawyers with him.
- He had no time to get to know the chiefs or the situation in NZ.

William's long-term problems

- As Governor he got no money from Britain to help him govern.
- He had to deal with Pakeha settlers demanding to buy Maori land, and saying they were scared Maori would attack them.
- It still took months to communicate with the British government. More than six months after William died, people in the British government were still talking about maybe removing him from his job.

How?

There was a lot of work done around Waitangi on 4 February 1840. William Hobson and James Busby had given Henry Williams, the missionary, the treaty draft to translate into Maori by the next day. Henry's brother William, the language expert, was away so Henry's son Edward helped. There is no evidence of any Maori help. Maori rangatira were also busy, at a hui at Taurangatira. Taurangatira is the place where Maori sat and thought about the treaty discussions for the next day. A stone seat was built to mark this place at Te Tii Marae.

challenges

1 Look at the picture of William:

(a) How old was William when he died?
(b) What challenges did he face in NZ?
(c) What season was it when he arrived in NZ and how comfortable would his uniform be?
(d) Name three places that were important for William on his voyage.
(e) Name the two places he made important as early capitals.
(f) How did William's actions shape the lives and experiences of others?
(g) At the time, William was criticised for not being a stronger governor. What do you know about him and his job that would make you more sympathetic to him?

2 Suggest a reason for each of the following facts:

(a) Nobody knows exactly how many Maori or Pakeha lived in NZ in 1840.
(b) Taurangatira is an important place for Maori.
(c) The British government's decision to make a treaty with NZ affected the lives of the people who were alive in 1840 and has continued to affect people's lives.

3 Copy the diagram (page 22) on why Britain needed to make a treaty. Can you add anything to the diagram to make it better? (A drawing? A funny saying?)

12

The Signing

Setting up a relationship between two groups

STEP 1

On 5 February 1840 William Hobson arrived at the beach, later called Hobson's Beach, off the HMS *Herald* at about nine in the morning. He and his party were dressed in their uniforms. It was a fine day and people were arriving in canoes, ships, and boats. William and his party walked up the track, later called Nias Track, towards James Busby's house. Outside James Busby's place, hawkers sold drinks such as rum and brandy, and foods such as pies and bread. James Busby's house faced the ocean. Gardens were on its left. Opposite the house was a marquee, about 50 metres long, made of ships' sails. Smaller tents were in a rough circle between house and marquee. Three mounted policemen in scarlet uniforms from New South Wales were on duty. Maori sat on the lawn smoking and talking. Many wore white feathers in their hair. Several taiaha, decorated with white dog-hair, crimson cloth and red feathers, were stuck into the ground. Some chiefs wore dogskin mats of black and white stripes; others wore coloured woollen cloaks. Some wore Pakeha clothes; others flax skirts. Hakitara, chief of Rarawa tribe, wore a silky white kaitaka mat.

STEP 2

William walked into James Busby's parlour and greeted James and Henry Williams. They put the final touches to the Treaty of Waitangi. Then William shook hands with the important visitors and settlers who filed in in their best clothes through the parlour and walked down to the tents.

STEP 3

At about 11 a.m. William and the official party of James Busby, officers and missionaries walked to the marquee. Flags decorated the inside of it. William's party sat down at a table on a raised platform in the middle; a British flag covered the table. William told the Pakeha what he was going to do; then he spoke to the chiefs in English and Henry Williams translated. This treaty is offering protection, he said. It is Queen Victoria's act of love towards you. He read the treaty in English; Henry Williams read out the Maori version. It was very short – it took less than one and a half minutes to read. It had a premable and three articles about the British Crown, Maori lands and possessions, and rights.

STEP 4

The chiefs spoke. A few wanted to sign the treaty but most didn't. They complained about Pakeha trade deals, lying, cheating, cursing, stealing, and land buying. If the Governor stays, said a chief, we'll be overrun with Pakeha and our land will be taken from us; we'll be slaves working for them, breaking stones and cutting wood like the prisoners at Port Jackson. Another chief said that if the new government stayed Maori dignity would be lost; they would be as low as worms. Some wanted to go back to before Pakeha brought blankets, bread, muskets and disease. Hone Heke changed his mind. Too late to send them away now, he said. Tamati Waka Nene said, 'Had you spoken like that when the traders and grog sellers came – had you turned them away – then you could well say to the Governor, Go Back … but now as things are no … Governor! You must preserve our customs and never permit our land to be taken from us.' The meeting was adjourned. The chiefs were invited to meet two days later for more talk. The official party went to Busby's house before going to dine on HMS *Herald*; Maori camped on the flat land near the Waitangi River mouth, down on the beach front marae, for more korero.

STEP 5

The next day a boat arrived at the ship for William. About 300–400 Maori were at Waitangi, he was told. Food was running short. William, still in his civvies and surprised to hear about this meeting, put on his dress hat and climbed into the boat. At the marquee, he said there was to be no more discussion; he would only take signatures to the treaty.

STEP 6

Henry Williams read the treaty in Maori. The French Roman Catholic Bishop Pompallier, who wore a purple gown and huge gold chain and crucifix, asked for and was given a public guarantee to Maori for free toleration in religion. William Colenso, the missionary's printer, asked if the chiefs understood the treaty and suggested they needed more explanations. Henry Williams brushed this aside. He told the chiefs the treaty was a sacred contract binding on both parties. But no chiefs came forward to sign it. James Busby suggested calling them individually starting with Hone Heke who was in favour of signing. Hone Heke signed. Hobson shook his hand and gave him two blankets and some tobacco. He said the Maori words he had learnt: 'He iwi kotahi tatou' ('We are now one people'). Other chiefs followed, adding their signatures or marks, or putting their moko, the pattern of their tattoo, on the parchment. HMS *Herald* gave a 21-gun salute.

STEP 7

NZ became a colony of Britain, which meant British law applied in NZ. The British appointed a governor, William Hobson, until he died in 1842, to live in NZ as the representative of the Crown seeing Queen Victoria was not coming to live here. The British Union Jack became the official flag and flew on Maika Hill at Kororareka.

challenge

1 Look at the picture of the treaty signing:

(a) What flags can you recognise?
(b) Which flag has been used to cover the two tables?
(c) Who is the chief in the white kiataka mat most likely to be?
(d) Which person is William?
(e) Why is William not wearing his official uniform?
(f) What Maori did William Hobson speak as he shook hands with the chiefs?
(g) What is the chief using to sign the treaty?
(h) In what different ways did chiefs sign the treaty?
(i) What shows that the treaty signing was an official and special time?
(j) Who is the chief, probably the first to sign, shaking Hobson's hand?
(k) Why was he the first to sign the treaty even though he was not the most important chief there?
(l) What are the objects on the smaller table to the right of the treaty likely to be?
(m) Queen Victoria did not come out from England to sign this treaty; who represented her?
(n) What is the object on the big table in front of Hobson's left hand?
(o) Which figures are most likely to be missionaries?
(p) Only the Crown signed the treaty, so why were the other Pakeha there?

13

Differences

The two groups experienced the same event differently

What happened to the treaty after the signing at Waitangi?

The mission press at Paihia printed copies of the treaty. Several copies were taken by ship around NZ so other chiefs who were not at Waitangi could sign.

A week after Waitangi, William Hobson and his staff met about 2000–3000 Maori at Hokianga. Some chiefs were against the treaty but about 56 signed it after William said, through his interpreter, that if they didn't, they would lose their lands to the untrustworthy Pakeha he had been sent to govern. He said that the Crown would protect their lands.

A female poet who was a Ngati Toa leader called Topeora signed the treaty in May 1840 when Henry Williams took it to Kapiti. Other females signed it too.

Major Bunbury and soldiers on the HMS *Herald* continued to take the treaty around NZ for several months. This was a hit and miss affair. Many chiefs in Taranaki, Hawkes Bay and the Wairarapa were not even asked to sign. Some chiefs like Te Wherowhero of Waikato refused to sign.

Henry Williams travelled to the west coast of the North Island, between Wellington and Wanganui, and to the Marlborough Sounds to persuade other Maori to sign the treaty.

The treaty was between the British Crown and Maori chiefs. In its travels around NZ, it was signed by Maori chiefs, not by Pakeha.

Te Rangi Topeora, chieftainess of Ngati Toa, signed the treaty in Kapiti in May 1840. She wears a cloak and tiki. In her hair are four tail feathers of the huia bird (now extinct) – this is a sign of high rank.

Why Maori chiefs signed the treaty:

- "Not many British settlers will come to live in NZ."
- "The chiefs will keep their mana and authority."
- "The treaty is a sacred bond between the chiefs and Queen Victoria."
- "Queen Victoria will control the number of British coming to NZ."
- "We'll be able to sell land to whomever we want."
- "The chiefs and Queen Victoria will have equal power."
- "Queen Victoria is getting only governorship of NZ."
- "Queen Victoria will control her criminals in NZ, especially those who break Maori law and set a bad example to Maori."
- "British rule will apply only to Pakeha, not to Maori as well."
- "The British say they won't harm Maori natives the way native people in other countries like Australia have been harmed."
- "Our land will be protected."
- "Britain will help Maori against France or others who try to conquer us."
- "We need to make sure no rival tribe steals a march on us by signing."
- "It will help us fight the Pakeha land sharks."
- "Maori will have the same rights as Pakeha."
- "Pakeha will bring the goods we need."
- "The missionaries say we should sign."
- "NZ won't become a British possession."

There were mix-ups in understanding what the treaty said because:

- two different cultures and two different languages meant two different ideas about what the treaty said
- Henry Williams' translation of the treaty into Maori wasn't the best
- there seems to have been only one Maori version but at least five different English versions being taken around NZ for signing. The Maori version does not match accurately any of the English versions.
- not all Maori chiefs signed the treaty
- no Pakeha from NZ signed it.

> 'What we have to say against the governor, the shadow of the land will go to him but the substance will remain with us.'
> Nopera Pana-kareao
> Te Rarawa leader

Examples of a mix-up in understanding:

- In the First Article, the English version said the chiefs give sovereignty (highest authority) to the Crown – Queen Victoria. But Maori did not have a word that meant *sovereignty*. So Henry Williams used *kawanatanga*, which was a word the missionaries had made up. The closest translation of it is *governorship*. Henry could have used either *mana* (standing or authority) or *rangatiratanga* (power to rule and make laws) instead of kawanatanga. They are both better translations of sovereignty. But if he had used either of those words, probably no chief would have signed. They would not have agreed to give up their mana or rangatiratanga.
- In the Third Article the Crown promised Maori royal protection and full citizenship. Pakeha thought this would bring British laws into NZ. Maori thought this would bring law and order among the British settlers.

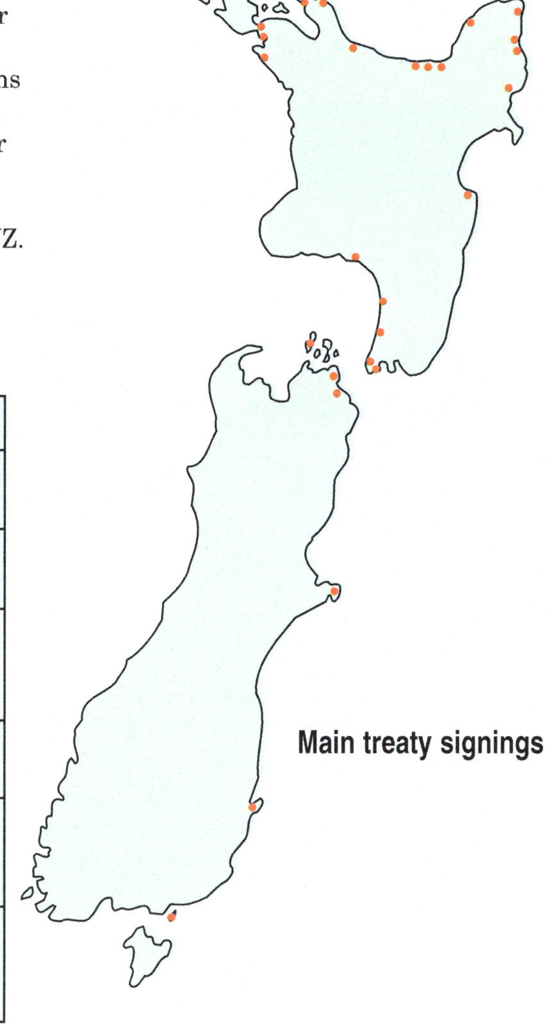
Main treaty signings

Differences in how Maori and Pakeha viewed the treaty

through Pakeha eyes	through Maori eyes
• set up a legal relationship between the British Crown and Maori chiefs	• set up a spiritual relationship between Queen Victoria and the Maori chiefs
• was a piece of paper with some signatures on it	• was a living document with special names on it
• meant the Crown would rule all NZ, which meant all Pakeha and all Maori	• meant the Queen would be like a governor and Maori chiefs would keep their mana
• meant British law would apply to everyone – Pakeha and Maori	• meant the Queen would use her law only to stop Pakeha being lawless in NZ
• meant Pakeha could now bring their culture, such as language and ways of doing things, into NZ	• meant Maori would keep their own culture and it would be safe in their own country
• meant Pakeha would buy land cheaply and turn NZ into a little England – a place of farms and towns	• meant Maori would keep all their lands, forest, fisheries, and other property

challenges

1 The map shows the places of the main treaty signings. Your job is to label some of them.

(a) Make your own copy of the map.

(b) Write the names of the following places (where the treaty was signed) on the right place (approximately) on the map:

Wanganui	Gisborne	Akaroa
Tauranga	Otago	Opotiki
Manukau	Queen Charlotte Sound	Cloudy Bay
Ruapuke Island	D'Urville Island	Tokomaru
Coromandel	Kaitaia	Whakatane

(c) Give three facts about where the treaty was signed. For example: Most signings took place on the coast.

2 The treaty signing is an example of the ways in which past events influenced relationships between groups involved in those events.

(a) Why is it called a 'past event'?

(b) Which two groups signed the treaty?

(c) Which group was the indigenous or native group of NZ?

(d) Which group was from another country?

(e) Was the treaty a written or an oral (word of mouth) treaty?

(f) Was the treaty written in English, or in Maori, or in both languages?

(g) Did the treaty mean the same to both groups?

3 Look at the reasons chiefs signed the treaty. Include Nopera Pana-kareao. Choose a reason and prepare a short talk about why you, as a very important chief, signed.

14

Challenges

Challenges and crises that people faced

The stories of Maketu and Hone Heke show how two cultures clashed.

The European name for Motuarohia is Roberton Island.

In 1841, a widow called Elizabeth Roberton was living at a place called Motuarohia. Her household included her eight-year-old son, her two-year-old daughter, her manservant, and a young girl who was the grand-daughter of Rewa, a Ngapuhi leader. Elizabeth had also hired a boy of about 16 called Maketu to work on her farm. Maketu was the son of Ngapuhi chief Ruhe.

The manservant was mean to Maketu and one day kicked him during an argument. Maketu killed the manservant by splitting his head open with an axe. He killed Elizabeth – he explained later that she had sworn at him. He killed the two girls. He chased the boy across the island and threw him over a cliff. He took refuge at his father's village.

Hundreds of Maori gathered to talk about it. Only one leader – Hone Heke – spoke against handing Maketu over to the British government. Ruhe gave up his son to avoid war with Rewa.

British law in Auckland tried Maketu, convicted him, and hanged him. Maori said they didn't object to Maketu's punishment but his hanging was drawn out and cold-blooded; Maori law would have killed him immediately, probably with a mere. Heke's followers carved a figure of the Governor and tied a noose around its neck.

Hone Heke (Hone is Maori for John) welcomed the British settlers but thought the British government was not honouring the treaty. He thought missionaries had tricked Maori into signing it.

Maori were used to their own laws but some British laws were hard to figure. Why put someone in prison for stealing a shirt? Why fine someone for being drunk but let the person who sold the drink go unpunished? Hone Heke thought British laws were hurting Maori and taking away the mana of the chiefs. The British government was forcing its policies on Maori who should rule themselves. He was also upset when William Hobson shifted the capital to Auckland, which meant the Bay of Islands was no longer the centre of trade, and settlers left the Bay to go to Auckland.

He started to fly an American flag on his war canoe when Americans living at the Bay told Maori how bad the British were and how cruel they had been to the Aborigines in Australia. He saw the British flag as the symbol of the British so he decided to get rid of the flagpole on Maika Hill.

Maori cut the flagpole down on Maika Hill four times in 1844 and 1845 even after the British covered the new flagpole with iron for the lower 20 feet and had two blockhouses to guard it.

Heke found an ally in a chief called Kawiti. Fighting between them and the British soldiers left Kororareka a smoking wreck. This led to war in the north, 1845–46. On one side were Hone Heke, who had about 300 men, and Kawiti who had about 150 men. On the other side were British troops (more troops were sent from Sydney; and the Governor had over 1000 men) and other Maori chiefs such as Tamati Waka Nene who had about 400–500 men.

Maori cut down the flagpole on Maika Hill four times.

Some of Hone Heke's thoughts and ideas:

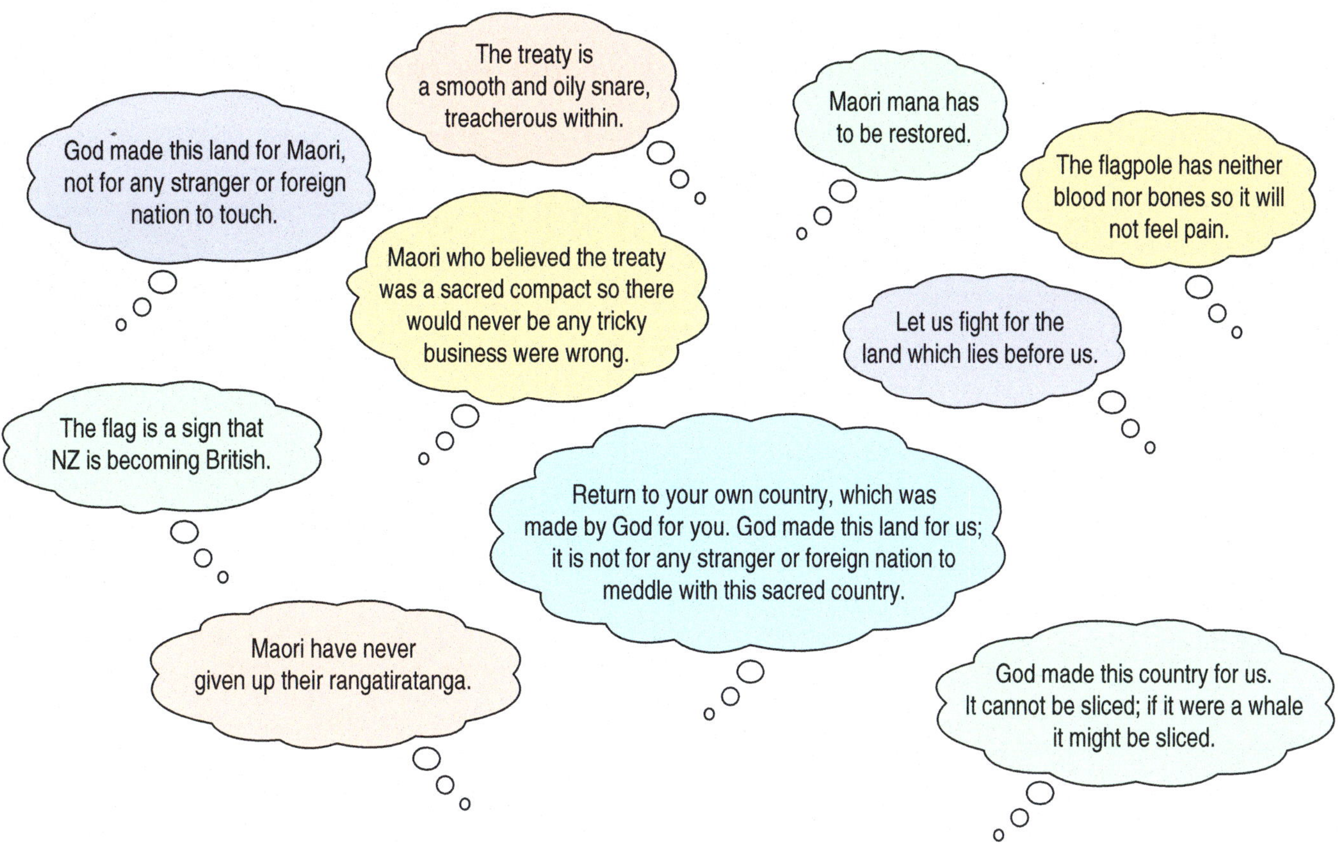

challenges

1 **Try making some sketches or a cartoon strip about the story of Maketu.**

2 **Look at the picture of the flagpole chopping:**
(a) Where is the flagpole situated?
(b) What are the Maori using to chop it down?
(c) Which flag is shown?
(d) What is happening to the flag?
(e) How are the Maori dressed?

4 **Look at Hone Heke's thoughts and ideas:**
Use some or all of them to help you create a full-page collage about Hone Heke's opinion on how the treaty was going.

5 **Heke's challenge:**
(a) How did Governor Hobson's decision to shift the capital away from the Bay of Islands to Auckland affect people's lives?
(b) What reasons would Hobson have had for shifting the capital to Auckland?
(c) One thing Hone Heke's protest was about was wanting social justice. How did his attitude over the Maketu affair show he thought Maori were not getting that from the British?
(d) What form did Hone Heke's protest take?
(e) How did the British government react to Hone's challenge?

Hone Heke (middle) with his wife Harriett, and Kawiti.

15

War

War is about important places, events, people, culture, and human rights

(Top) Painting by John Lewin: Attack by British forces on Ohaeawai pa in 1845.

(Bottom) Painting by Lance-Sergeant John Williams: A scrap between British forces and Maori at Okaihau.

In the war in the north there were several scraps between the two sides. They fought only during the day and sometimes stopped by agreement.

The war proper consisted of the British troops attacking Heke and Kawiti at three important pa:

1 Puketutu, in May 1845 (the pa was not captured and Heke and Kawiti were not caught)
2 Ohaeawai, in June 1845 (Maori left the pa)
3 Ruapekapeka, in January 1846 (British took the pa but Maori had deliberately left the pa).

The battle at Ohaeawai

Hone Heke and Kawiti went to Pene Paui's pa at Ohaeawai. The British force of almost 600 men led by Colonel Despard landed at Onewhero Beach and marched up to the Kerikeri Mission while the HMS *Hazard*'s blue-jackets brought guns and stores up the Kerikeri River by boat. The force then marched through Waimate to Ohaeawai, and camped 500 yards (about 500 metres) from the north face.

Kawiti had strengthened the pa and doubled its size. He had three rows of palisading timbers and an inner fence of heavy puriri logs. He put in hidden rifle pits, trenches and anti-artillery bunkers.

On the 24 June, 8 a.m., the British big guns opened fire. Although they fired all day, the pa held. Colonel Despard called for a 32-pounder gun from HMS *Hazard*. Six days later it arrived. Next day it opened fire. While it bombarded the pa, a group of warriors crept out. They circled through the puriri forest and surprised the Maori allies and British soldiers protecting a gun on Puketapu Hill. They shot a soldier, seized the gun, and hauled down Tamati Waka Nene's flag.

Colonel Despard was furious. He said the 32-pounder would have loosened the puriri timber palisades so a storming party would be able to take the pa. His junior officers advised against it. Tamati Waka Nene was also worried. But the Colonel was stubborn. He ordered a storming party to parade, and the troops were given a midday meal.

The troops formed up in the valley about 100 yards from the stockade. They waited. Behind them guns threw shot and shell into the pa. Half an hour later the bugle blared: Advance!

The soldiers raced up the slope. The warriors in the pa were safe in trenches. Only the muzzles of their guns poked out from under the palisade. Other warriors were hidden behind the palisade with their guns firing from loopholes. British soldiers fell; many died. The bugle command rang out: Retire.

For days the British kept bombarding the pa while they loaded wounded soldiers into carts and stretchers to go back to Waimate.

On the morning of 11 July 1845 they found the pa deserted; Maori had left during the night. It was the custom to leave a pa after blood had been spilt.

Colonel Despard ordered his troops to destroy the pa. He could not believe Maori did not have Pakeha help in building such a wonderfully strong pa. Three days later the British packed up and marched to the Mission Station at Waimate. Many of the survivors were going to have to fight in the final battle at Ruapekapeka Pa in January 1846. That battle would end Hone Heke's war in the north.

The British had been unable to totally beat Heke and Kawiti and the Governor granted Heke and Kawiti free pardons. British troops had learned to admire Maori military and engineering skills, but their government still wasn't listening to Heke and Kawiti, who were saying the Maori chiefs wanted the partnership and human rights they believed the treaty would give.

In 1858 a gang of Maori supervised by Kawiti's son chopped down a spar in the bush, dragged it to Kororareka Beach and worked on it until it looked like a mighty flagpole. Four hundred Maori dragged the pole up the hill and raised it. The British flag floated at the top of it. The pole was called Whakakotahitanga, which means 'being at one with the Queen'. When war erupted in the 1860s, the tribes in the north did not fight.

challenges

1 Look at the battle pictures:

(a) The people fighting in such battles did not have cameras to record what was happening. Lance-Sergeant J. Williams and John Lewin painted these watercolours. In what ways are they different to a photograph?
(b) What was the British uniform like and how suitable for the NZ bush was it?
(c) What do the pictures suggest about how battles were fought at that time?
(d) What sounds would both sides have been hearing during these battles?
(e) Why did troops who were attacking a pa need shelter?
(f) Where did Maori fighting the British live during the battle?

2 The war of the north:

(a) Which two groups of people fought each other in the war of the north?
(b) What was the relationship between those two groups during the war?
(c) What was the relationship between those two groups after peace was made?
(d) In what way was Hone Heke giving a political challenge to the British government?
(e) Why was the war in the north a crisis for the British government?

3 The following are answers to questions about the battle at Ohaeawai. What could the questions have been?

(a) Colonel Despard (b) HMS *Hazard* (c) Kerikeri
(d) Kawiti (e) puriri (f) Puketapu
(g) Waimate (h) Ruapekapeka

4 You can visit Ohaeawai today and read about the battle on a plaque inside the church there. This is where the battle information on this page came from.

(a) Why was Ohaeawai an important place for strategic (military planning) reasons in 1845?
(b) Why was Ohaeawai an important place for cultural reasons in 1845?
(c) Why is Ohaeawai an important place for historical reasons today?
(d) Why is Ohaeawai an important place for individuals today?
(e) NZ historian James Belich wrote a book and presented a television programme about the 19th century wars including the war in the north. What two ways has he used to help people find out about places?
(f) How is the plaque a way of recording the past?

5 Different views:

(a) Give one way the actions of Hone Heke and Kawiti helped shape the lives and experiences of others.
(b) How would people like Colonel Despard and Governor Grey have seen them at the time?
(c) How do modern historians tend to see them?
(d) Why is there this difference?

16

Kingitanga

Causes and results of a 'new' political system

An important event was the beginning of Kingitanga – the Maori King movement. It had causes and results.

Causes of the event

Population By 1858 more **Pakeha** than **Maori** lived in NZ.

Parliament Britain gave NZ its own parliament in 1852. Only men were allowed to vote in the elections. They had to own land individually and so hardly any **Maori** could vote. Everyone in parliament was **Pakeha** – there were no **Maori**.

Treaty of Waitangi **Maori** thought of the Treaty of Waitangi as a living treaty or sacred treaty. It had the name or tohu of the chiefs on it. But **Pakeha** were not interested in it. They had not signed it. Besides, they were busy learning to survive in the new land.

Unity Some **Maori** decided to have a King, the same as **Pakeha** had Queen Victoria, to unite the tribes. The person was to: *hei pupuri i te mana* – hold mana of the people; *hei pupuri i te whenua* – hold the land; *hei puru i te toto* – stop the flow of blood.

Land **Pakeha** settlers wanted to buy land faster than **Maori** wanted to sell it. They looked at what they thought was unused **Maori** land and asked why the government didn't make it available for **Pakeha** settlement. They wanted to clear the land of forest and plant grass seed to make farms. But many tribes sold all their spare land and said they were not going to sell any more. However, some members of a tribe might want to sell land while other members didn't.

The main man of the event

Maori chose **Te Whero Whero** of Waikato as King.

He was living in Manukau in 1840 when the treaty came down for signing. He refused to sign it but he was friendly towards the Pakeha government and was one of the chiefs who sold land to the government in the Manukau area. However he protested to Queen Victoria over the 1846 instruction that all land not actually occupied or cultivated by Maori was to be regarded as Crown property. He said it was against the guarantees of the Treaty of Waitangi.

He had mana whenua (land) because Waikato had a famous mountain called Taupiri; burial grounds of ancestors mentioned in songs, poems and stories; the Waikato River, which was the mother of the tribes.

He had mana kai (food) because the Waikato had good plentiful foods.

He had mana tangata (human) because his family was connected with leaders of all the main ancestral canoes; his father was the leading tohunga of the tribe. He had been a great warrior. He was said to have killed 150 prisoners with his mere in 1831 when he led an expedition into Taranaki.

This boundary post was near the Bell Block in Taranaki where fighting broke out. Katatore, who had been against selling the Bell Block to Pakeha, put it up.

Results of the event

- Te Whero Whero was crowned King in Rangiaowhia in 1857 and was installed at Ngaruawahia in 1858. He took the name of Potatau.
- Soon he had his own courts, a flag, troops and constables.
- When he died in 1860 his son Tawhiao became King.
- Not all tribes supported the Maori King idea. Those who did were most of the tribes from the Waikato, King Country, Western Bay of Plenty, and Taupo districts and some other tribes like Ngatiruanui of Taranaki. After war broke out against the government in Taranaki in 1860 the Atiawa also joined Kingitanga.
- Kingitanga was sending a message to the Pakeha government. We're not anti-Pakeha and we see the King as being with the government, not against. But you've shut us out of political decisions and we want to control our own destiny. We want to keep the traditional authority of chiefs and we want to stop land sales to the Pakeha. We don't want the king to rule over the tribes but to bring the chiefs together to make laws for all. We want to live at peace with the settlers but we want to live on our own lands in our own way.
- Pakeha were against any movement they saw as stopping them getting land.
- Meetings in the middle of the North Island organised a tapu on selling land within certain boundaries. Maori put up boundary posts to mark the limits of Pakeha land in Taranaki and the Waikato. But in some tribes, there were still arguments because some Maori wanted to sell land, and some didn't. Pakeha land agents sometimes put pressure on Maori to sell by promising to build hospitals and schools or set up reserves of Maori land, if they did.

These are some symbols (things that stand for something) Maori used for the idea of Kingitanga.

challenges

1 Look at the picture of the settler's cottage:

(a) What belongings of the settler can you see in the picture?
(b) What would the settler have had to do to the forest before he could build this home?
(c) Where would the settler get his water supply?
(d) What dangers to the settler might the forest threaten?
(e) From where would the settler get his knowledge about events in the rest of the country?
(f) How much time would the settler have to think about issues such as the Treaty of Waitangi?
(g) What would be the main thing the settler is thinking about?
(h) In what ways was the settler keeping his culture alive in his new country?

Before the Pakeha settlers could start making a farm out of the forest, they had to clear a patch and build a house for the family.

2 Look at the picture of the boundary post:

(a) What did a boundary post look like?
(b) Why did Maori put them up?
(c) What traditional weapons are the Maori holding?
(d) The buying and selling of land after the Treaty of Waitangi was an important event. Which two cultural groups were involved in it?
(e) How was that event influencing the relationship between the two groups involved?
(f) Why did Pakeha want to buy Maori land?
(g) Why would some members of a tribe want to sell land?
(h) Why would some members of a tribe not want to sell land?

3 Make your own drawings of the symbols of Kingitanga.

4 Look at the picture of Te Whero Whero:

(a) Give five facts (things that are true) you can get from this picture.
(b) Kingitanga was a response to a crisis Maori faced – what sort of crisis was it?
(c) How did some Maori work together to face this crisis?

Land Again

War over the most important resource – land

In 1859 at a meeting in Taranaki of Maori and Pakeha and the Governor, a chief called Te Teira offered to sell land that the Pakeha settlers wanted at Waitara. Another chief, called Wiremu Kingi (Te Rangitake), said he would never let the land be sold. The chiefs had personal history. Te Teira blamed Wiremu Kingi for the refusal of a young woman to marry a relative of his to whom she had been promised; she married Wiremu Kingi's son instead. Te Teira believed his family was wronged and that the compensation offered by Wiremu Kingi was not enough.

The Governor got two land buyers to carry out a private enquiry. They said Teira had the right to sell. So the government gave Teira some money, and sent surveyors to Waitara. Wiremu Kingi sent a few old women to pull up the surveying pegs. On Sunday 4 March 1860 British soldiers marched out from New Plymouth to attack Wiremu Kingi's pa at Waitara.

When the British attacked Wiremu Kingi's pa at Waitara, it began a series of battles between some Maori on the one side, and British troops helped by some other Maori on the other side. These battles were between 1860 and 1872. They are part of what is sometimes called the land wars. Another term for them is the New Zealand wars, even though the battles took place only in some places in the middle of the North Island.

When Wiremu Kingi died in 1882, said to be over 90 years old, Pakeha blamed him for these troubles in Taranaki and called him a 'rebel'. In 1927, long after the government had got control of the Waitara land, a Royal Commission (a group set up to check out an issue) said Wiremu Kingi and his people were not rebels and they had no choice but to fight in self-defence. In 1936 a carved house, Te Ikaroa-a-Maui, was opened at Manukorihi pa in Waitara. A representation of Wiremu Kingi Te Rangitake stands at the front of the house.

Areas of fighting and/or unrest in the NZ wars:

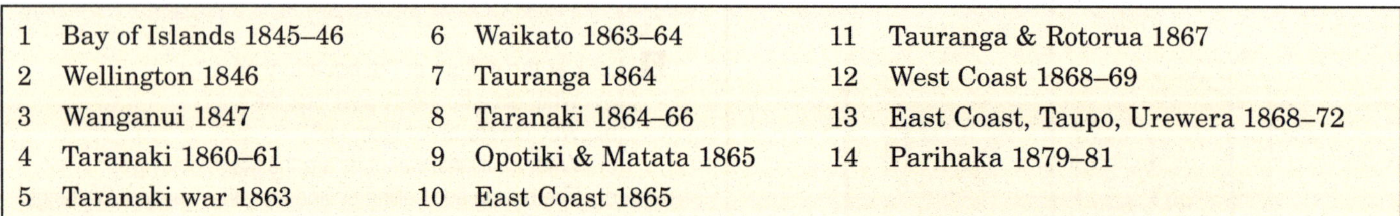

1	Bay of Islands 1845–46	6	Waikato 1863–64	11	Tauranga & Rotorua 1867
2	Wellington 1846	7	Tauranga 1864	12	West Coast 1868–69
3	Wanganui 1847	8	Taranaki 1864–66	13	East Coast, Taupo, Urewera 1868–72
4	Taranaki 1860–61	9	Opotiki & Matata 1865	14	Parihaka 1879–81
5	Taranaki war 1863	10	East Coast 1865		

Causes of wars

Both sides thought they could win. Maori had seen the British heavy uniforms and gear, and ancient methods of warfare. But the British had been involved in many colonial wars to squash 'rebellious natives'. They had reserves of military power and knew Maori were not united – some Maori, called kupapa or 'friendlies', ended up fighting on the British side. (When the British troops pulled out of NZ, the forces left fighting were called colonial or government forces.)

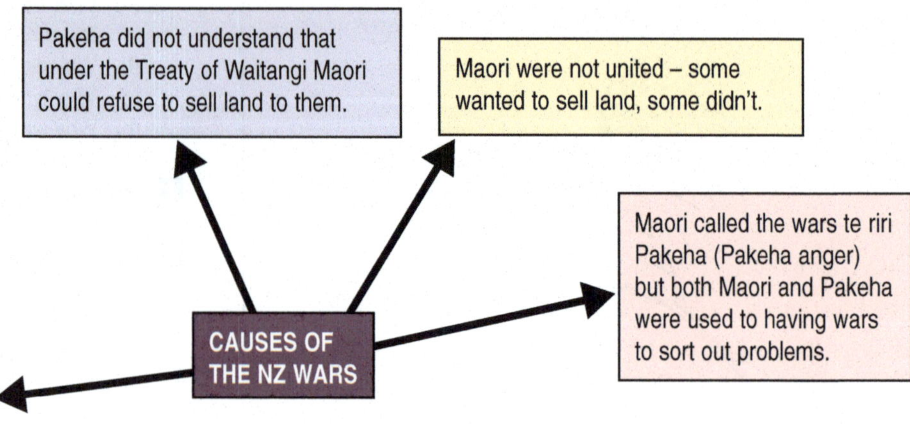

Armies

Maori had tupara – double-barrelled percussion shotguns that were better than the British Enfield at close range although no match for the bayonet in hand-to-hand fighting. They lacked money to buy food and ammunition, but were clever and fast, knew the land and had strong pa. Their guerrilla warfare could pin down British soldiers in blockhouses. But their small forces were up against a professional, well-drilled, experienced, and well-led British army.

General Cameron led this 1863 attack in Taranaki in revenge for an ambush of British troops; Pakeha writers and artists at the time wildly exaggerated the size of the defeated Maori force.

Then and now

At the time people saw General Cameron as being slow and timid, and a poor leader who lost battles because he lacked inspiration. Maori called him 'The Lame Seagull' because of the British way of building long saps towards pa. Later Cameron resigned and went home to Britain. He had begun to think the war was being fought for settlers to get more Maori land. Today many historians say he was the best British commander to serve in NZ.

A famous place

At Orakau pa, Maori fought for days against bayonet charges and artillery fire, with raw potatoes to eat and wooden bullets to fire. Rewi Maniapoto said, 'Let us abide by the fortunes of war. If we are to die, let us die in battle.' Hauraki Tonganui said, 'Friend. I shall go on fighting you for ever and ever' ('E hoa, ka whawhai, tonu ahau kia koe ake, ake'). Some women in the pa who refused General Cameron's offer for them to leave were killed. Ahumai Te Paerata said, 'The women and children will stay with the men and fight. We will die with our men.'

challenges

1 Look at the map of Taranaki:

(a) What is your relationship to Taranaki? (Live there? Visited? Heard about it? Seen a picture of it?)
(b) On what coast is Taranaki?
(c) What is the name of the city in Taranaki?
(d) How many European place names are on the map?
(e) Where is Waitara in relationship to Egmont/Taranaki?
(f) Why were most Maori settlements around the coast?
(g) Why would this area have been a special place to Maori?
(h) Why did Pakeha settlers want to buy the land?
(i) How was Waitara an example of how Maori were not united?

2 Look at the picture of the 1863 engraving:

(a) Nobody had a camera here so what possibilities for mistakes in this drawing are there?
(b) Why did artists of the time often draw Maori pa as easy to knock over, even though they weren't?
(c) Why were pa important to Maori?
(d) Why have battle sites become important to both Pakeha and Maori today?
(e) Why would particular battle sites have become important to individual Pakeha and Maori?
(f) If William Hobson and the chiefs who signed the Treaty of Waitangi had been watching this battle, what might they have thought?

3 The NZ wars:

(a) Which two main groups of people fought each other in the wars?
(b) Name a leader from a group.
(c) How did some people see that leader at the time?
(d) How do some people see that leader today?
(e) How would the wars have influenced relationships between those groups?
(f) Why would different battles have been important for different communities?
(g) Why would the battles have been important for NZ as a country?
(h) In what way were the wars a crisis for Maori?
(i) In what way were the wars a challenge for the British?
(j) How had Maori warriors been trained to help in such a crisis?
(k) How had British soldiers been trained to help in such a challenge?

18

Raupatu

An event that has shaped relationships up to today and possibly in the future

Confiscation of Maori land

War had already wrecked Maori crops, animals, churches, and houses when the government passed laws to confiscate Maori land. This confiscation was called raupatu. It was punishment for Maori who were said to have 'rebelled' against the government, and it was a way to open up more land for Pakeha settlers. The government made mistakes; it took land from some tribes who hadn't fought, it took land from some tribes who had fought *for* the government, and it didn't take land from Ngati Maniapoto, who had supported the King movement. Raupatu was in some places in the North Island. The South Island was busy with gold rushes and setting up huge sheep stations. The only politicians who objected to the British invasion of Waikato were from the South Island – they were concerned about how much the use of so many troops would cost.

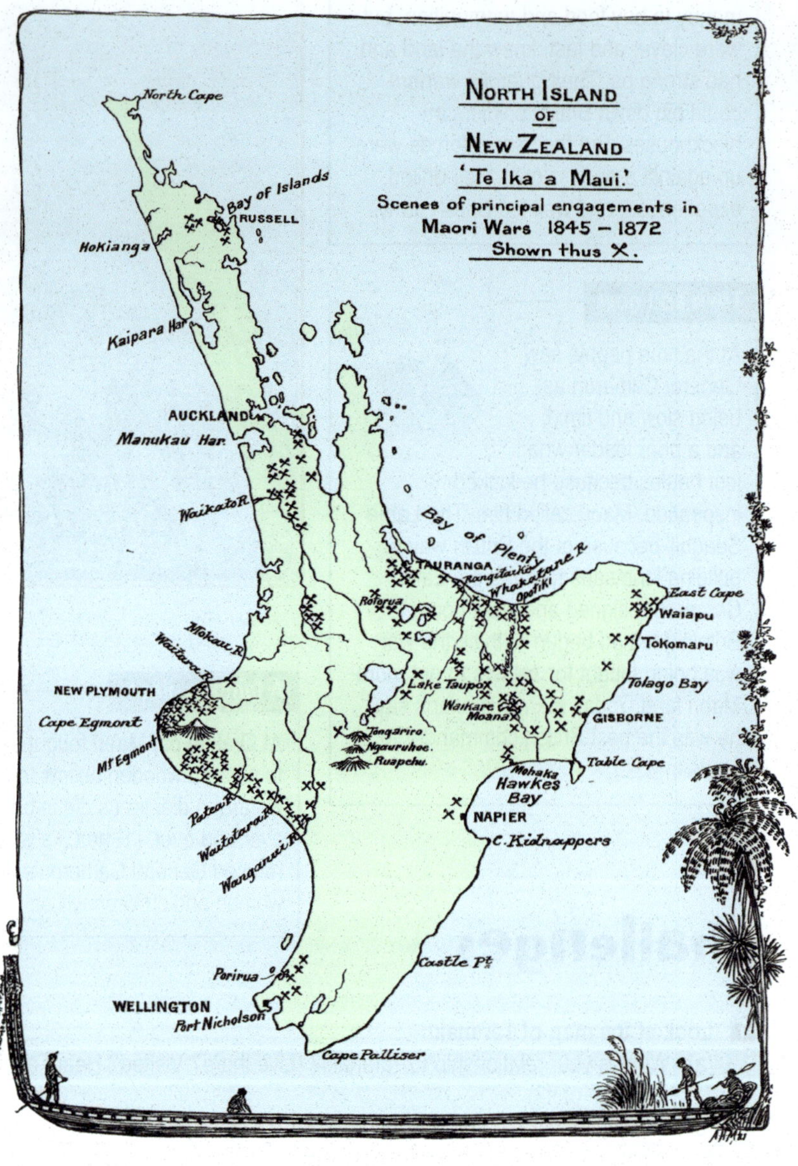

Raupatu is still affecting the relationship between some Maori and Crown today. It made Maori say they were more scared of the Pakeha's peace than his war. They said if it had only been blood spilled and the land left alone, the trouble between Maori and Pakeha would have been over long ago. It meant some people had to shift from their lands. Tuhoe, for example, lost the fertile flat lands of the Bay of Plenty and moved back into the harsh hill country of the Urewera. Waikato tribes had to go south into Ngati Maniapoto territory. This became the King Country. Their village, Tokangamutu, was the beginning of today's town called Te Kuiti. The Maori King stayed there until 1881. Then he came out and put his gun down. He said: 'The killing of men must stop, the destruction of land must stop. I shall bury my patu in the earth and it shall not rise again.'

Tauranga
Opotiki
AUCKLAND
Gisborne
TARANAKI
WELLINGTON
HAWKES BAY
Napier

Areas Confiscated

Under the Settlements Act 1863
Area 3,490,106 acres
(about 1,413,000 hectares)

Under the East Coast Land Titles Investigation Act 1867
Area about 1,240,000 acres
(about 502,000 hectares)

How people saw those who were involved in the 19th century NZ wars is not always the same as how people today see them. Some examples are groups such as Hauhau, and individuals such as Te Kooti, Titokowaru, and Te Whiti. Raupatu played a big part in their lives and helped shape their actions and ideas.

The Hauhau

One day in about 1826, Waikato raided Taranaki and captured a young boy called Te Ua and his mother. They took him to Kawhia as a slave. Later he went back to Taranaki and in the 1860s he founded a religion called Pai Marire, which meant 'good and peaceful movement'. He called his church Hauhau because Te Hau, the spirit of God in the wind, carried the news to the faithful. His followers became known as Hauhaus. They believed if they shouted 'Pai marire! Hau! Hau!' during a battle, Pakeha bullets wouldn't hurt them.

At this time an Anglican missionary called Carl Volkner lived at Opotiki. He sided with the government in the war against Maori. His congregation of Te Whakatohea warned him not to come back to Opotiki from a trip to Auckland but he came back with missionary Thomas Grace. Maori took them prisoner and the next morning, 2 March 1865, hanged Carl from a willow tree. An hour later they took Carl's body down and cut the head off. Some people tasted blood or smeared it on their faces. Kereopa Te Rau, a Pai Marire leader, forced out the eyes and swallowed them. He said one eye was parliament and the other was the Queen and English law. Kereopa got mana from this and later became known as Kaiwhatu (the Eye-eater).

The killing outraged Pakeha. From then on they called any Maori who opposed the government Hauhaus, regardless of what religion they were. They said Te Ua was mad. The government sent military expeditions to Opotiki to look for Carl's killers. They arrested some locals and executed some, including Chief Mokomoko. The government confiscated a large area of land from Maori 'rebels'.

In 1872 the government captured Kereopa. There was no direct proof of his responsibility for the killing but a Pakeha witness testified he had seen Kereopa among those who escorted Volkner to the willow. Kereopa was hanged. At the time the government saw Kereopa as a savage bloodthirsty ruffian and Volkner as an innocent brave missionary. Today it is thought that Kereopa's wife and two daughters were killed when the British burned Rangiaowhia near Te Awamutu in 1864, and the next day he saw his sister killed. Letters that Volkner sent to the Governor prove he was acting as a spy for the government and there is acknowledgement that Whakatohea people knew their missionary had acted as a government spy and that he had ignored their warnings not to go back to Opotiki. Chief Mokomoko has been pardoned and the Crown has apologised for calling Whakatohea 'rebels'.

Hauhau prisoners captured near Wanganui.

challenges

1 Raupatu:

(a) What two groups of people were involved in raupatu?
(b) Why would raupatu have affected the two groups in different ways?
(c) How would raupatu have influenced relationships between those groups?
(d) Why did raupatu continue to shape relationships between the two groups up to today and possibly in the future?

2 Give one:

(a) way the government decision to confiscate land affected people's lives
(b) example of a shift of population because of raupatu
(c) way the shift to a new place would have affected the people concerned
(d) way the shift to a new place would have affected the place left behind
(e) way the shift to a new place would have affected the place to which they moved
(f) reason the King Country is important to Maori today
(g) reason the King Country is important to Pakeha today.

3 Look at the map of battles:

(a) Was a battle fought anywhere near where you live?
(b) Why is only the North Island shown?
(c) In what parts of the country were the main battles of the war fought?
(d) Name four mountains on the map.
(e) Today the wars are called the NZ wars. What did they used to be called?

4 Look at the map of confiscations:

(a) What does confiscation mean?
(b) Have you ever had anything confiscated from you?
(c) What sort of things do groups such as schools and police confiscate from people?
(d) At what times/dates did the government make the raupatu confiscations?
(e) What two acts of Parliament made the confiscations?
(f) What was the total area confiscated?
(g) When was land confiscated in Taranaki?
(h) When was land confiscated in the Gisborne area?
(i) When was land confiscated in the Waikato area?
(j) When was land confiscated around Opotiki?
(k) When was land confiscated around Tauranga?
(l) When was land confiscated around Napier?

5 Name:

(a) a crisis that Carl Volkner faced
(b) a challenge that isolated Pakeha settlers faced
(c) a crisis that Kereopa faced
(d) a crisis that Chief Mokomoko faced
(e) a crisis that Te Whakatohea faced.

19

Resistance

People whose actions shaped the lives and experiences of others

Te Kooti around the East Coast

In 1866 Te Kooti was fighting on the East Coast on the side of the British but they accused him of being in touch with the Hauhau. Te Kooti denied it and said he was a 'Queen's Maori'. He wrote letters demanding a proper trial but the British shipped him off to the Chatham Islands without one. There he studied the Bible and started a new religion called Ringatu, which means the Upraised Hand.

In 1868 Te Kooti and his friends grabbed a schooner and escaped back to NZ. They killed about 54 Maori and Europeans at Matawhero near Gisborne, including some Maori chiefs. Government forces besieged Te Kooti at an ancient hilltop pa called Ngatapa. The people in the pa got down the cliff by vines and escaped. The government forces captured about 270 of them in the Urewera bush and shot 120 males. Government troops chased Te Kooti through the North Island for years. He finally gave up his struggle against British colonists in 1872.

At the time many Pakeha and Maori feared and disliked Te Kooti. They described him as a criminal, a murderer, and a rebel, and spoke of the 'massacre' at Matawhero. Many historians today say Te Kooti was a charismatic leader and a gifted guerrilla fighter who suffered injustice. They point out government revenge at Ngatapa.

Te Kooti.

Titokowaru at Taranaki

'My mother is dead,' said Titokowaru, 'but I was nourished by her milk. Let our land be kept by us as milk for our children.' A peacemaker and leader of non-violent resistance, he was also a general who won a series of victories against the colonial troops 1868–69 during his campaign to get back the confiscated lands of Taranaki. He wrote to the British Colonel he was fighting, 'You were formed a pakeha; and England was named for your country. We are Maoris with New Zealand for our country. There has been fixed between you and us a great gulf, the ocean. Why did you not take thought before you crossed over to us? We did not cross hence over to you. Away with you from our land to your own country in the midst of the ocean.' Titokowaru was never defeated in battle but for some unknown reason, his followers slipped away in 1869. One theory is he ran out of food or ammunition; another theory is he had an affair with another man's wife.

At the time Pakeha were terrified of him and called him a 'rebel'. Today it is known that at least five times he spared enemy Pakeha, and some historians say he is the most brilliant general NZ has produced; it is generally seen that he was fighting to defend his land and way of life.

This engraving from the Illustrated New Zealand Herald of 1 December 1868 shows troops fighting Maori at Titokowaru's pa Ngutu-o-te-manu. On 7 September 1868 Titikowaru destroyed a colonial army at Te Ngutu-o-te-manu, and on 21 August fought again here; the battle was called a draw but some say Titokowaru won again. Titokowaru had rebuilt the village of Te Ngutu-o-te-manu near Pungarehu, just north of the Waingongoro River, as his base. It had houses, a large marae and a beautiful meeting house. It was originally a centre of peace.

Te Whiti at Parihaka

Te Whiti, along with his brother-in-law Tohu, became famous for his non-violent protest against raupatu at a Maori village called Parihaka in Taranaki. It was built on confiscated land. The government had promised reserves for Maori when it took the land but there was no sign of them. Te Whiti's idea was to occupy the confiscated lands, at least until the reserves were set aside for Maori.

In 1879 government surveyors appeared on the confiscated Waimate Plain; Te Whiti's followers told them to go. Small bands of Maori arrived at confiscated land occupied by Pakeha settlers and ploughed up their paddocks. The government arrested the ploughmen, who went peacefully off to jail. Other ploughmen arrived and continued ploughing.

The Native Minister Bryce (a Pakeha) and hundreds of Armed Constabulary (police) built a road to Parihaka. They tore down fences but Maori followed them and fixed the fences. The Constabulary arrested the fencers, who went quietly while other fencers took their places.

On 5 November 1881 Bryce, mounted on a white charger with sabre and full military uniform, led armed troops, volunteers and Armed Constabulary on to the marae at Parihaka. 'Arrest Te Whiti and Tohu,' he ordered. 'Destroy the village.' Maori call this day of each year Parihaka Day.

At the time, the government saw Te Whiti and Tohu as acting against them and would not allow official documents about Parihaka to be published until later. Today it is seen that the government used troops to put down a non-violent protest. More people are learning about what happened at Parihaka. Recently there was a big exhibition about it in Te Papa.

Te Whiti.

challenges

1 Name:

(a) a political challenge that the government faced
(b) a crisis that Te Kooti faced
(c) a crisis that Titokowaru faced
(d) a crisis that Te Whiti faced
(e) a government decision that affected people's lives
(f) a method Maori used to get social justice and human rights
(g) a way the government reacted to Maori efforts to get social justice.

2 Look at the engraving of Titokowaru's battle:

(a) If you had seen the picture in the *Herald*, which side would you have picked as the winner?
(b) Which side was the winner?
(c) List things about battles in the 1860s that seem 'peculiar' today.

3 Look at the pictures of Parihaka:

(a) What differences would there be between Parihaka in 1881 and today?
(b) To whom is Parihaka likely to be an important place?
(c) Why are more New Zealanders learning about Parihaka today?

4 Then and now:

(a) Name a person or group from this chapter whose actions have shaped the lives and experiences of others.
(b) How were their actions seen at the time?
(c) How are their actions seen today?

Parihaka in the 1880s.

Parihaka today.

20

Results

Two cultures experience the treaty event differently

Ways Maori looked for social justice after the NZ Wars and ways government reacted

1 Visits to the Queen Maori groups went to England to try to get the Queen to listen to their pleas for social justice. Chiefs had signed the Treaty of Waitangi with the Crown and they believed they had a personal relationship with the Queen. In Maori eyes the treaty had come before NZ got its own government in 1852; so it was the most important. But in Pakeha eyes, the British had given the job of looking after Maori to the NZ government. Maori groups who went to London did not get to see the Queen. For example in 1882 a group of Ngapuhi chiefs went to England to ask for a Maori Parliament to stop Pakeha ignoring the Treaty of Waitangi. Officials told them it was a matter for the NZ government, not the Queen. Even King Tawhiao, who led a party of chiefs to England in 1884 to get the Treaty of Waitangi honoured, did not get to see the Queen.

The crown was a symbol of royalty. When people talked about the Crown, they meant the King or Queen as the head of the British government.

2 Parliament When Maori organised their own parliament at Waipatu in Hawkes Bay in 1892, it had no power because the NZ government refused to recognise it.

3 Bill In 1894 Maori tried to introduce a Maori Rights Bill into Parliament so Maori could control their own lands and fishing; Pakeha members walked out.

4 Laws Government passed laws to make it easier for Pakeha to buy Maori land. An example was the law that set up a Native Land Court with judges sitting on it.

The Native Land Court

Its main job was to work out which tribes owned what land, then divide the land up among individual members of the tribe and give them certificates of ownership – this made it easier for Pakeha to buy land.

→ Any Maori could apply for a land right and all the other owners of the land had to go to Court to give evidence of their ownership; when they didn't go they lost the land.

→ Court business cost a lot of money – Maori owners had to pay for land surveys, and legal costs.

→ Maori had to travel to town where the Land Court sat, and run up debts for food, accommodation, and lawyers. They might have to sell land to pay their debts.

→ Some land agents were sharks; they lent money to a group of claimants to make a claim, using the land as security. When Maori couldn't pay off the debt, the agent got the land.

→ Sometimes a few of the hapu took land applications to the Court without the rest of the hapu knowing and so they were the only ones who got the right to sell land to Pakeha.

→ Maori with land often found

- it was hard making farms because they lacked money, skills and suitable land
- it was useless trying to keep land now Pakeha were passing all those laws, and so they sold it
- banks did not want to lend money to Maori farmers
- government passed laws to lend money to Pakeha to settle and develop farms, but not Maori.

→ When the land was gone Maori

- had to earn money to survive
- got poorly paid jobs such as shearing on Pakeha farms, or felling bush for public works.

Maori population went down

The treaty didn't figure for Pakeha because most didn't know about its history, and it wasn't part of any law passed by Parliament so courts didn't have to recognise it. To most Pakeha the treaty was past history, and nothing to do with them. They also thought Maori weren't going to last and talked about smoothing the pillow of a dying race. Maori population shot down to less than half what it had been when James Cook arrived because:

- thousands had died in the musket wars between the tribes before the treaty
- some had died in the NZ wars against the British
- traditional cures did not get rid of the new diseases
- they still had little resistance to Pakeha diseases such as flu
- they were poor and so their living conditions were poor
- the loss of their land put them in low spirits
- alcohol became a problem for some
- they did not have good access to doctors or medicine – people who went to hospital had to pay and Maori could not pay; even if they could, they didn't like being put in a ward away from the whanau; nor were they always welcome – e.g. in 1906 only four doctors in the Waikato would take Maori patients

Many Pakeha had thought Maori should be turned into brown-skinned Europeans as quickly as possible for their own sakes. That relationship is called **assimilation**. The relationship that lets two cultures have equal rights is called **biculturalism**.

challenges

1 Look at the pictures of the Pakeha house (below) and the Maori village (below left):
How many differences can you find?
How many things the same can you find?

2 Out of the two groups – Pakeha and Maori – which one:

(a) got land?
(b) lost land?
(c) got political power?
(d) lost political power?
(e) brought their culture in from overseas and set it up in NZ?
(f) had to struggle to keep their culture alive in NZ?
(g) built up grievances (complaints) about the treaty after 1840?
(h) did not build up grievances about the treaty after 1840?
(i) tried to get the Crown in England to listen to their grievances?
(j) tried to get their own parliament in NZ?

4 Give:

(a) a reason Maori looked for social justice and human rights
(b) a way Maori tried to get changes in relation to social justice and human rights
(c) a way the lack of change in social justice affected the lives of Maori
(d) a way the government could have helped Maori get social justice
(e) a way the relationship between Pakeha and Maori at this time was not biculturalism
(f) an example of discrimination against Maori
(g) an example of both cultures being treated equally by an individual
(h) an example of a problem that needed a solution.

5 Refer to the picture of Queen Victoria:
What things show she was a person of high mana?

Problem Solving

Looking for social justice for Maori

Towards the end of the 19th century governments had started to look after Maori better. As well, Maori individuals and groups worked hard to help other Maori.

The Young Maori Party, educated at Te Aute College in Hawkes Bay, included leaders Apirana Ngata, Te Rangi Hiroa (Peter Buck), and Maui Pomare. They tried to improve Maori health and education and encouraged Maori to take on some Pakeha ways of doing things.

Some Pakeha ways, especially competition, did not work for many Maori. Instead they found leaders they trusted who followed the old ways such as working with each other and looking after the whanau. These leaders, many of whom worked out of the spotlight, told Maori there was hope for the future.

New Maori religions such as Ratana gave Maori hope for the future.

All Blacks like George Nepia, entertainers like Howard Morrison, opera singers like Kiri Te Kanawa, became heroes to all Kiwis.

In 1900 the government appointed a Maori Health Officer – Maui Pomare. He travelled to Maori villages all over NZ. He encouraged people to put in new wells, pipe drinking water to houses, dig rubbish pits, build airier houses. Sometimes they let him burn their old huts.

Protest groups made all Kiwis aware of Maori issues. An example was Nga Tamatoa (The Young Warriors) set up in the late 1960s. It challenged the Crown over failing to honour the treaty such as not protecting Maori land and language.

Princess Te Puea of Waikato was a positive role model. Her mother was the eldest child of King Tawhiao; she died when Te Puea was 15. Te Puea decided to move the King's village back to Ngaruawahia and call it Turangawaewae – a place to stand. She showed Maori could help each other and look after their culture; she showed the usefulness of some Pakeha ways such as proper sewerage and education. She was against government making Waikato Maori sign up for the First World War. At the time the government was impatient and saw her actions as defiant and disloyal. Today she is seen as having great mana and is honoured for making Kingitanga strong again.

In 1960 Government made Waitangi Day a national day;
1973 Government made Waitangi Day a national holiday.

Governments began to spend money on Maori housing, district high schools, loans to farmers, giving back some land.

In 1975 a Maori hikoi (march) from Northland to Parliament in Wellington took the message that Maori had only about 3 million acres (about 1 million hectares) left from the 66 million they held in 1840.

There were individual protests such as that of Eva Rickard at Raglan (Whaingaroa). During the Second World War government took some tribal land for an aerodrome. After the war, instead of going back to the local tangata whenua as promised, the land went to the local council who leased it to the Raglan Golf Club. Eva and her people began peaceful protests at the golf course and after nine years, government returned the land.

An important protest was at Bastion Point in Auckland. There the chief of Ngati Whatua had been pressured to sell land to the Crown. But before he died he got 280 ha kept for his people. But governments kept taking bits until in 1951 the tribe was evicted from its papakainga (home territory) on the Okahu Bay foreshore, and went into state houses at Orakei. In 1976 the Crown said it was to develop the land for luxury housing and parks. Ngati Whatua demanded the return of the land; government refused but didn't do the development. In 1977 Maori protesters occupied Bastion Point for 506 days until the government sent police and army to evict them and destroy their buildings and gardens.

In the 1980s government adopted an official policy of biculturalism, which meant making Pakeha and Maori cultures of equal importance.

Waitangi Tribunal

Another way the government tried to get social justice and human rights for Maori was the Waitangi Tribunal – Te Ropu Whakamana I Te Tiriti o Waitangi.

WHEN? The government set it up in 1975.

WHY? To check out Maori claims and grievances.

WHO? Sixteen members plus Chairperson; about half Maori, half Pakeha.

WHAT? Checks out Maori claims that government has done things against the treaty and hurt Maori; can recommend how to fix things.

HOW? Claimants must be Maori; claims can only be against laws or Crown, not against private individuals; can hear claims about private land but generally cannot recommend it be taken away from owners; government does not have to do what tribunal recommends.

WHERE? Tribunal can meet anywhere.

Members of the Waitangi Tribunal delivering the report on the Chatham Islands.

tribunal = group appointed to hear and settle disputes
grievance = a real or imaginary complaint
claim = saying something like 'this land is mine'
claimant = a person who makes a claim

RESEARCH: When people take a claim to the tribunal, they have to get their claim properly researched. That is one way people find out about places and history, and how they record cultural practices and heritage, and pass it on to others. The tribunal likes to see or hear any of the following:

- written history (mana whenua) giving information about the iwi, hapu or whanau, rohe (regional) boundaries, sites of special significance such as wahi tapu (sacred) or mahinga kai (food sources)
- oral history such as traditional stories, histories about how the Crown actions affected the claimants
- maps and photographs
- written history reports researched by professional historians from Maori Land Court minute books, the National Archives, missionary letters, whakapapa (genealogy) records, published tribal histories.

challenges

1 Find the name of:

(a) relationships that can exist between cultural groups
(b) a famous college
(c) the man whose English name was Peter Buck
(d) the religion started by Te Kooti
(e) the Maori term for Waitangi Tribunal
(f) the Maori Health Officer in 1900
(g) a Maori protest group of the late 1960s
(h) a Maori All Black
(i) the national holiday set up in 1973
(j) the Waikato Maori princess
(k) the female protester at Raglan Golf Club
(l) the Maori word for march
(m) the Maori word for home territory
(n) the Maori name for Raglan
(o) a group appointed to hear and settle disputes
(p) the Maori King's village.

2 Look at the cartoon:

(a) When was the cartoon published and how many years ago is that?
(b) Which fish stands for Pakeha and which one stands for Maori?
(c) Why would the cartoonist have chosen these two fish as symbols?
(d) Which one makes the suggestion to integrate?
(e) What is going to happen next?
(f) The cartoon was making a comment that Maori at the time thought that Pakeha had so far not made a great effort to get biculturalism going. How has the cartoonist shown this?
(g) Use the information in the cartoon to finish this sentence: Integration means ...

'The shark and the kahawai were swimming one day when the shark said, "Let's integrate." When the kahawai agreed, the shark opened its mouth and swallowed the kahawai.' This old joke is how a Secretary for Maori Affairs last century showed what Maori thought of the so-called biculturalism.

Waitangi Tribunal

The role of Government in getting people's human rights

If you have never experienced it yourself, imagine how the claimants feel when finally the tribunal starts hearing their claim. It might have taken more than a hundred years to get someone to listen. Maybe the young people of the tribe, the rangatahi, perform a haka. Speakers tell the tribunal how government decisions have affected their lives; they may mention some or all of the following: (Ⓢ= social results; Ⓔ= economic results; Ⓟ= political results)

being forced from their land hurt them and attacked their mana Ⓢ

teachers punished children for speaking Maori at school Ⓢ

they had been made to feel like second-class people Ⓢ Ⓟ

being forced from their land stopped them working together as a tribe Ⓢ Ⓔ Ⓟ

they feel bad because they could not stay to protect their land and keep home fires burning on it Ⓢ Ⓔ

they had to work for Pakeha as labourers Ⓔ

at school the tipuna were taught only skills suitable for servants Ⓢ

only a few people of the tribe today speak Maori as their first language Ⓢ

they need to hear they are the kaitiaki, the guardians, of the land Ⓢ Ⓔ Ⓟ

there has been crime and family violence Ⓢ

they have had below average incomes, higher unemployment Ⓔ

young people leave school today with no qualifications Ⓔ

this is their chance to heal and head into the future as a whanau Ⓢ

this is their journey home, the way of facing past problems and getting solutions Ⓢ

the tipuna were put down because of their skin colour Ⓢ

they are not asking for the return of any land in private ownership Ⓔ

they are not asking for the return of all land that the government took through raupatu Ⓔ

many people had to resettle elsewhere and lost track of their original whakapapa Ⓢ Ⓔ Ⓟ

they need to hear they are not rebels as the government called them in the1860s Ⓢ Ⓟ

the hapu has always talked about the loss of land Ⓔ

this may be the first time an old person has been on the marae to meet the whanau Ⓢ Ⓟ

they are not asking for the return of land that has roads or houses built on it Ⓔ

they were brainwashed into taking the blame for the NZ wars Ⓢ Ⓟ

the tribe has suffered disease, early deaths, drug and drink addiction Ⓢ

For Waitangi Tribunal claims, NZ is divided into 15 Rangahaua Whanui districts:

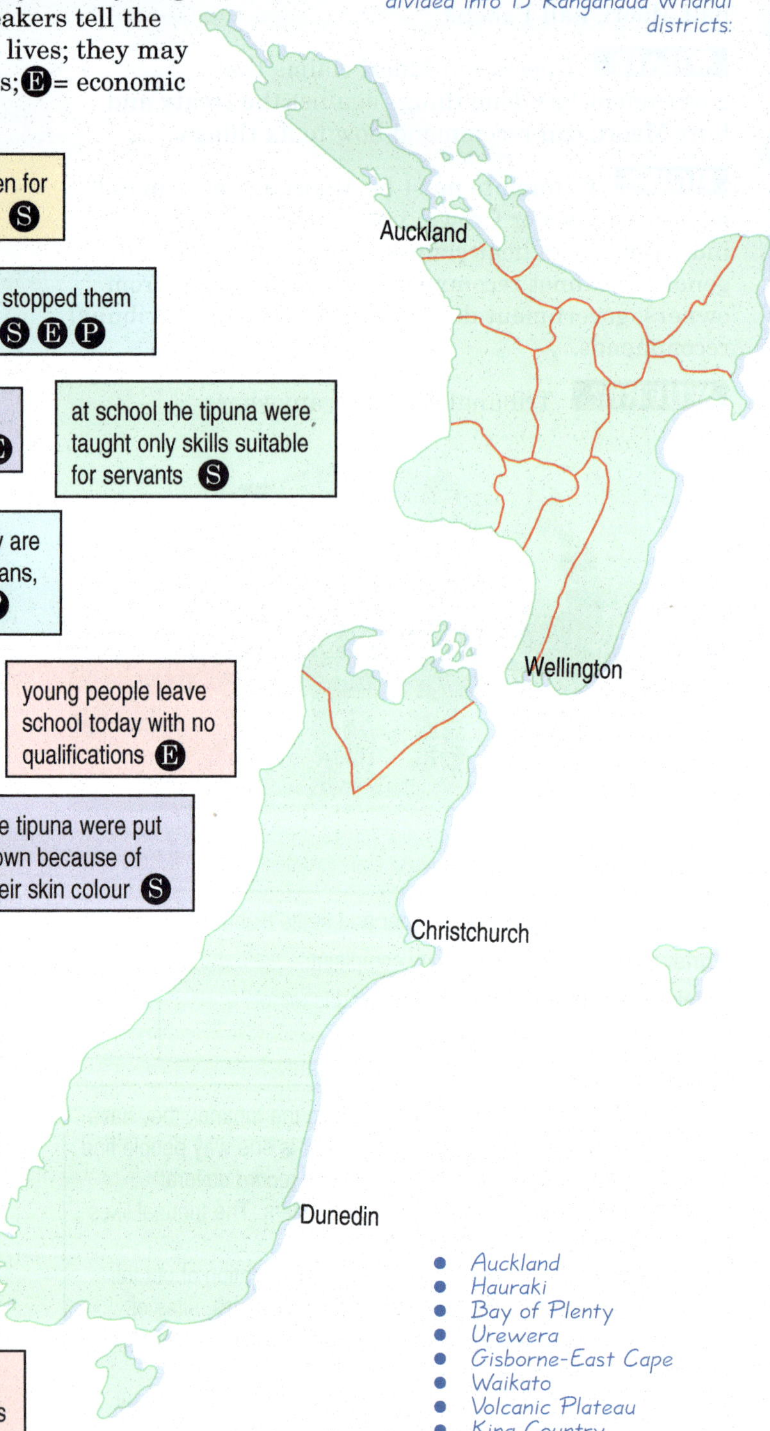

- Auckland
- Hauraki
- Bay of Plenty
- Urewera
- Gisborne-East Cape
- Waikato
- Volcanic Plateau
- King Country
- Whanganui
- Taranaki
- Hawkes Bay-Wairarapa
- Wellington
- Northern South Island
- Southern South Island
- Chatham Islands

The tribunal has heard hundreds of claims. The first big one was Tainui in Waikato, about raupatu. The Deed of Settlement in 1995 had an apology for the Crown's past unjust actions and a payout of $170 million made up of land and money.

Another big settlement was the Ngai Tahu Deed of Settlement in 1997 in the South Island. It included payment of money and land worth $170m, an apology from the Crown for past dealings which hurt Ngai Tahu, and the restoration of many Maori names for mountains and other places.

Maori leaders said the apology was to do with past actions and no one was suggesting present day New Zealanders should take it personally. The NZ Prime Minister went on to Takahanga Marae at Kaikoura on the day of signing the settlement. He talked about the journey that the nation had been on since the signing of the treaty 157 years ago, and how some governments had paid little attention to the spirit in which the treaty had been signed, while others, probably with good intentions, tried too hard to 'make us all one people'. Once Pakeha and Maori listened carefully to each other, they found that fair and sensible solutions were possible.

Name: Kaituna River claim
Where: Bay of Plenty
When: 1984
Claimant: Ngati Pikiao
Reason: they were worried about a proposed pipeline to put waste into Kaituna River, which is used for fishing and has spiritual and economic importance to them
Tribunal finding: agreed with claimants
Recommendation: use other ways to get rid of waste
Result: Crown agreed with tribunal's recommendations.

Examples of claims the tribunal has heard:

Name: Orakau
Where: Auckland, near the centre of city, between Hobson Bay and Mission Bay
When: 1984
Claimant: Joe Hawke and 12 others on behalf of Ngati Whatua
Reason: said Crown wrongfully took 700-acre (280-hectare) Orakei block
Tribunal finding: Crown breached (broke) treaty when it bought Orakei instead of keeping it in tribal ownership; the protesters at Bastion Point broke the law by trespassing
Recommendations: Return some of the land to Ngati Whatua
Result: Government agreed; paid $3 million to Ngati Whatua.

Name: Motunui
Where: Taranaki coastline and Waitara River
When: 1983
Claimant: Aila Taylor of the Puketapu and Te Atiawa hapu, Taranaki
Reason: synthetic fuel plant proposed coastal outfall at Motunui could harm kaimoana
Tribunal findings: discharge of waste at Motunui threated kaimoana and harmed mana of people because they could not show usual hospitality of giving seafood to visitors
Recommendation: fuel plant should get rid of waste on land, not in ocean
Result: Crown agreed to follow tribunal's recommendation.

Name: Maori language claim
When: Waitangi Tribunal's Te Reo report released 1985
Where: for all tribes
Claimant: all Maori
Reason: claimants said Crown had failed to protect and encourage Maori language; said Maori should be an official language
Tribunal finding: critical of government policy towards Te Reo
Recommendation: language should be legal in courts, government departments, and public bodies
Result: Maori an official language; kohanga reo, kura kuapapa, Maori and bilingual classes and units.

challenges

1 Questions on raupatu to talk about in your group:

(a) What was a cause of it?
(b) What were some social results of it?
(c) What were some economic results of it?
(d) What were some political results of it?
(e) Why would Pakeha and Maori have experienced it differently?
(f) Why would it have been important for particular communities?
(g) Why would it have been important to Maori culture?
(h) Why would it have been important to NZ generally?
(i) How would it have influenced relationships between the Crown and Maori?
(j) How is it continuing to influence the relationship between the Crown and Maori today?
(k) How might it keep influencing the relationship in the future?
(l) How was it linked with the Maori rights movements and protests?

2 Claims can involve big numbers. For example, in Taranaki:

- the government confiscated 1.2 million acres (485,600 hectares)
- tribes lost another 296,000 acres (120,000 hectares) through illegal purchases
- government land reform and Native Land Court took another 426,000 acres (about 170,000 hectares).

Add up the totals in acres and hectares.

3 Map-making:

(a) Make your own copy of the map on page 44.
(b) Include a key for your map (the Rangahaua Whanui districts are listed in the right order).

4 Find all the Maori words in chapters 22 and 23 and give their English meanings.

23

Treaty Today

Resources and the treaty

The experiences of native peoples when faced with another culture coming to live in the country, are different in each country. Aborigines in Australia faced bullets, flour poisoned with arsenic, their children being taken from them and brought up by whites. Indigenous groups from other countries visit NZ because their country does not have a treaty like the Treaty of Waitangi.

A sense of fairness, and of trying to put wrong things right is part of Pakeha culture. The need to be consulted about issues that affect the environment and resources is part of Maori culture. In 1991 a government Act called the Resource Management Act said that people making decisions about the environment and resources must take notice of the principles of the Treaty of Waitangi.

A principle is like a basic law or rule. The government made up the principles in 1989. They are not the treaty but they are ideas about how the treaty should work. The principles are:

- the right of government to govern and make laws
- the right of iwi and hapu to self-management and control of their resources
- the idea of partnership and a duty to act in good faith
- the duty of the Crown to protect tangata whenua in the use of their resources and taonga (treasures).

It's been saved from fire, gnawed by rats, stained by water, but the treaty is a survivor. Today you can go and see it in Wellington's Constitution Room, which is the home of Paths to Nationhood - Nga Ara Whakakotahi. The room is a walk-through history of NZ. In the middle of the room is the Treaty of Waitangi - Te Tiriti o Waitangi; it has the most important place because it is the founding document of modern NZ.

Some resources:

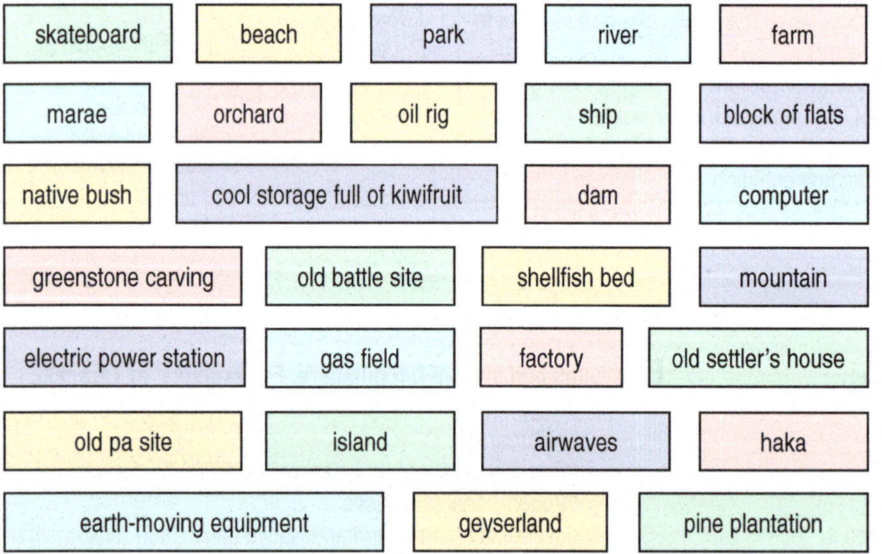

Today the Treaty of Waitangi, and the sharing of resources, are important issues in NZ. People can get heated talking about them. Sometimes they put labels on others. They use 'redneck' for a Pakeha who says things such as 'Maori are getting special treatment from the government and that's unfair', or 'the Treaty of Waitangi should be thrown away'. They use 'radical' for a Maori who says things such as 'Maori should control all the resources and Pakeha should go home to their country of origin'. A name sometimes used for NZ is 'the land of the long white frown'. Other labels are 'Uncle Tom' for a Maori who is seen to be favouring Pakeha, and 'bleeding heart liberal' for a Pakeha who is seen to be favouring Maori.

A 'moderate' means a Pakeha or Maori who tries to see all sides of an argument. Some Maori moderates say that while it is true that government took Maori land through raupatu, Maori also lost a lot of land because they sold it. Certain Maori leaders did well from this sale of the land. They say that while it is true that Maori used to be punished at school for talking te reo, it is also true that a petition from Maori leaders after the NZ wars asked that Maori children be taught only in English. They also say that life was tough before Pakeha arrived with new technology to enrich the tribes, and wars between tribes, especially the musket wars, killed thousands of Maori, far more than the wars against the British. They say Maori are survivors, not victims.

Some Pakeha moderates say the treaty can't be thrown away because it means so much to Maori. They say neither Pakeha nor Maori are going to leave NZ so things have got to be worked out so both are happy. They say NZ needs to become truly bicultural before it can talk about being multicultural and catering for other cultures such as Chinese. They say they do not believe they should be personally held responsible for all the problems that Maori face but they are pleased that the Waitangi Tribunal has started to help fix up the mistakes from the past.

A visit to the Maori Meeting House at Waitangi - the Whare Runanga - leaves you with the message: 'You are invited to bring in with you your anger, your discontent, your questions, but take with you the gifts of Rongo, Peace, Goodwill and Friendship.'

challenges

1 Special events

(a) In 1840 Mrs Busby celebrated the signing of the treaty by planting a pohutukawa tree beside the Treaty House. Name an event you might celebrate in the future by planting a tree.

(b) How might a visit to the special Whare Runanga at Waitangi help someone who was unhappy about the treaty?

2 Look at the resources in boxes on page 46. Name one that:

(a) Pakeha are likely to visit for 'historical' reasons
(b) Maori are likely to have a legend or old story about
(c) you might own as an individual
(d) Pakeha are likely to be attached to because it has passed down through the generations
(e) Maori are likely to think of as a taonga
(f) Pakeha are likely to think of as a treasure
(g) both Maori and Pakeha are likely to be interested in using
(h) is likely to be a special place for both Pakeha and Maori
(i) Maori are likely to think of as having a mauri or spirit
(j) is likely to need 'managing' because of possible effects to the environment
(k) is likely to be important for kaimoana.

3 Houses

(a) Sketch the outline of a house type that Pakeha introduced to NZ. Fill the shape with ideas of how a house is important to Pakeha culture (e.g. 'An Englishman's home is his castle').

(b) Sketch the outline of a Maori meeting house. Add things to it to show the house is like a person. Ideas: koruru (at top of roof) = head; maihi (bargeboards) = arms; raparapa (end of bargeboards) = fingers; amo (side boards) = legs; roro (entrance) = brain; tatau (doorway) = opening into body; tahuhu (ridge pole) = spine; heke (rafters) = ribs.

4 Land

Make up an icon (small symbol such as a tree) to stand for LAND. Around it put some ideas to show how and why both Pakeha and Maori cultures have become attached to land in NZ. For example a saying is 'You can take the child out of the farm but you can't take the farm out of the child.'

The Future

The treaty and the future

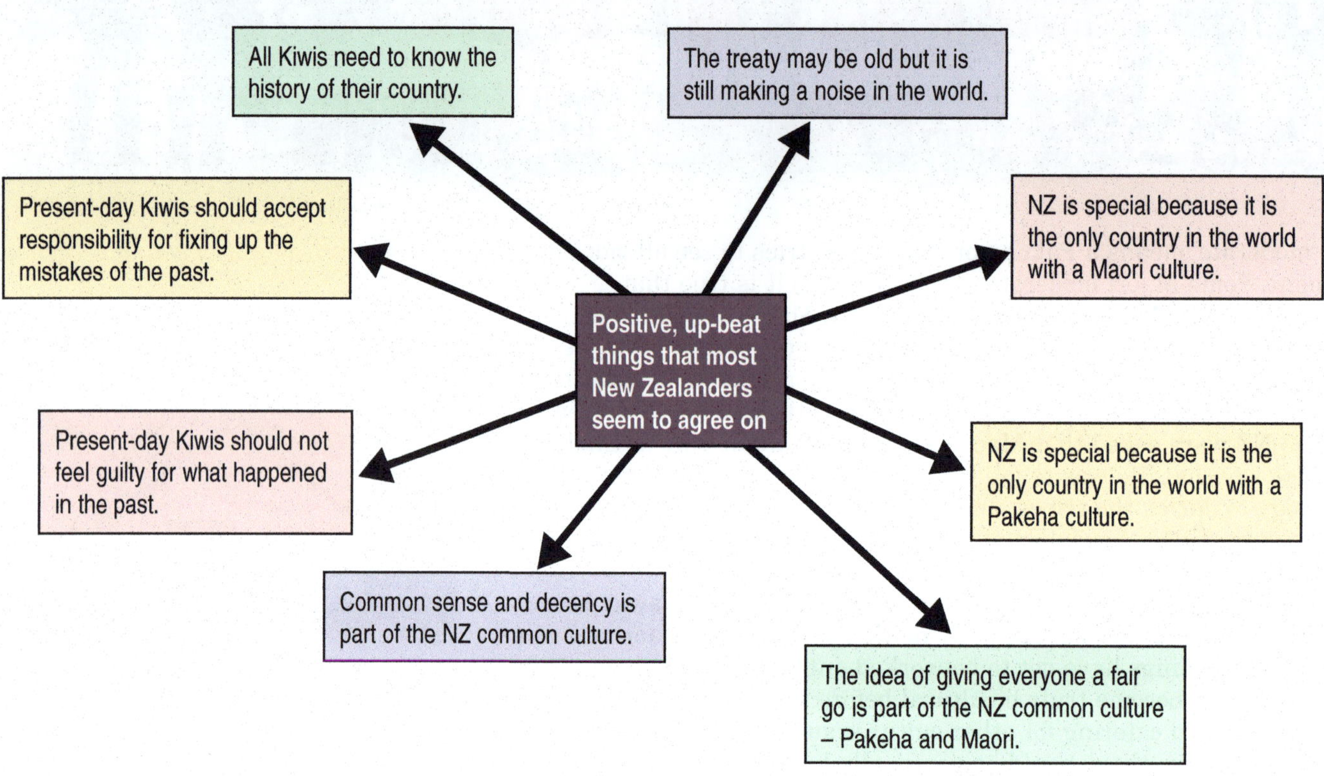

challenges

1 Show your opinion on how important it is to know about your country's past, by making one of the following about it:

- poster
- poem
- piece of writing
- drawing
- collage
- film/video
- home page for a website

2 Cartoon study:

(a) Say what your reaction is to the cartoon (what you think of it).

(b) Do you think it is true for people your age today? Say why or why not.